BASIC / NOT BORING
SCIENCE SKILLS

PHYSICAL
SCIENCE

Grades 6–8+

Inventive Exercises to Sharpen
Skills and Raise Achievement

Series Concept & Development
by Imogene Forte & Marjorie Frank
Exercises by Marjorie Frank

Incentive Publications, Inc.
Nashville, Tennessee

About the cover:
Bound resist, or tie dye, is the most ancient known method of fabric surface design. The brilliance of the basic tie dye design on this cover reflects the possibilities that emerge from the mastery of basic skills.

Illustrated by Kathleen Bullock
Cover art by Mary Patricia Deprez, dba Tye Dye Mary®
Cover design by Marta Drayton, Joe Shibley, and W. Paul Nance
Edited by Anna Quinn

ISBN 0-86530-376-2

3   4   5   6   7   8   9   10   07   06

PRINTED IN THE UNITED STATES OF AMERICA
www.incentivepublications.com

TABLE OF CONTENTS

CELEBRATE BASIC
SCIENCE SKILLS

Basic does not mean boring! There certainly is nothing dull about . . .

   . . . wandering around checking out the insides of atoms

   . . . being able to brag that you know your way around the Periodic Table

   . . . deciphering clues that identify mystery atoms

   . . . figuring out, once and for all, how to ace those problems about trains speeding in different directions

   . . . explaining quarks, isotopes, electron clouds, mirages, green flashes, and other curiosities of physics

   . . . learning your way around colloids like whipped cream, toothpaste, paint, and butter

   . . . finding out what's really happening when you bleach your hair or fry an egg

   . . . being able to explain why people don't fall out of upside-down roller coasters

   . . . telling the difference between X-rays, cosmic rays, microwaves, and radio waves

Celebrating the basics is just what it sounds like—getting excited about science because you understand more about how it works. The pages that follow are full of exercises for students that will help to review and strengthen specific, basic skills in the content area of physical science. This is not just another ordinary "fill-in-the-blanks" way to learn. The high-interest activities will put students to work applying a rich variety of the most important facts about many aspects of physics and chemistry. Students will do this work while enjoying fun, challenging exercises about atoms and compounds, forces and motion, light and color, electricity and magnets, mixtures and solutions, and a load of other great physical science surprises.

The pages in this book can be used in many ways:
- for individual students to sharpen a particular skill
- with a small group needing to relearn or strengthen a skill
- as an instructional tool for teaching a skill to any size group
- by students working on their own
- by students working under the direction of an adult

Each page may be used to introduce a new skill, reinforce a skill, or even assess a student's performance of a skill. There's more than just the great student activities! You'll also find a hearty appendix of resources helpful for students and teachers—including a ready-to-use test for assesssing these physical science content skills.

As students take on the challenges of these adventures with wonders in the physical world, they will sharpen their mastery of basic skills and enjoy learning to the fullest. And as you watch them check off the basic physical science skills they've strengthened, you can celebrate with them!

SKILLS CHECKLIST FOR PHYSICAL SCIENCE

✔	SKILL	PAGE(S)
	Define, describe, and draw the structure of atoms	10–14
	Identify, define, and distinguish between three states of matter	17–19
	Name and distinguish between physical and chemical properties of matter	17–22
	List names and properties of common elements; Compare elements	11–16
	Describe properties of different kinds (groups) of elements	15
	Define and distinguish between elements and compounds	10–20
	Find information on a Periodic Table	10–16
	Identify composition and formulas for common elements	11–16
	Define, identify, and give examples of organic and inorganic compounds	23–25
	Define and distinguish between acids, bases, and salts	23–25
	Describe the behavior of particles in states of matter and changes in states	17, 18
	Explain physical changes: melting, boiling, freezing, condensation, evaporation	18
	Define, describe, and give examples of mixtures, suspensions, solutions, colloids	19
	Distinguish between physical and chemical changes in matter	22
	Define light; Explain reflection, refraction, transparent, translucent, opaque	44–46
	Explain how a spectrum is produced	44–46
	Explain how mirrors and lenses work	47
	Explain how color is seen and why objects have color	45
	Define and describe waves; Diagram and explain features of a transverse wave	36, 37
	Define sound and vibrations; Describe properties of sound	38, 39
	Explain how sound travels	38, 39
	Define and describe concepts and terms related to heat	31
	Explain and give examples of static electricity	40, 41
	Define and describe electric current; Distinguish between kinds of current	42
	Describe and diagram parallel and series circuits	42
	Define electric power and calculate it in watts	43
	Describe features of radio waves, microwaves, X–rays, and gamma rays	36, 37
	Describe and define properties of magnets, including electromagnets	48
	Describe, define, and give examples of magnetic fields; Explain how they work	48
	Define and explain concepts, terms, and laws related to motion	27–30
	Calculate speed, time, and distance	30
	Define and give examples of forces	27, 32, 33
	Identify and explain six types of machines	34, 35
	Define and explain energy; Describe different forms of energy	29–33, 37, 40–43, 48

PHYSICAL SCIENCE

Skills Exercises

ON THE INSIDE

A Greek philosopher called Democritus, who lived over 2000 years ago, taught people that all things were made of grains which could not be divided. He called these grains *atoms* because in Greek *atom* means *indivisible*. Today, *atom* is the common name for the tiny particles of matter that cannot be further divided (and still be the same substance). If you could look inside an atom, you'd find that it looks like a miniature solar system, with something in the center and other things orbiting around it.

I. Label the parts of this atom (nucleus, protons, electrons, neutrons).

A. _____

B. _____

C. _____

D. _____

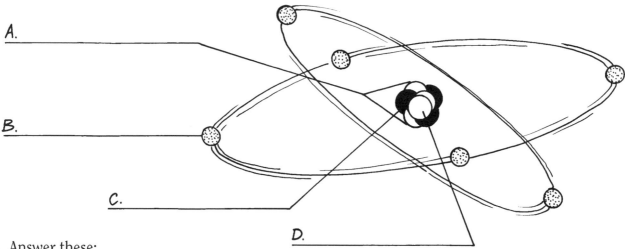

II. Answer these:

_____ 1. the part of the atom that carries no electric charge

_____ 2. the part of the atom that carries a positive charge

_____ 3. the part of the atom that carries a negative charge

_____ 4. the number of electrons that can be held in the first orbit (closest to the nucleus)

_____ 5. the number of electrons that can be held in the second orbit

_____ 6. the number of electrons that can be held in the third orbit

_____ 7. there are the same number of these two particles in an atom

_____ 8. the atomic number is the same as the number of these particles

> Draw your own model of an atom with eight protons, eight neutrons, and eight electrons (an oxygen atom).

Name _____

WHICH ATOM IS WHICH?

Every kind of atom has its own unique look. All the atoms of an element have this same look. Here's a chance for you to look at some atoms and tell what elements they are. Write the name of the element next to each atom. You may need to use the Periodic Table to help you out. (You can find one on page 52 of this book.)

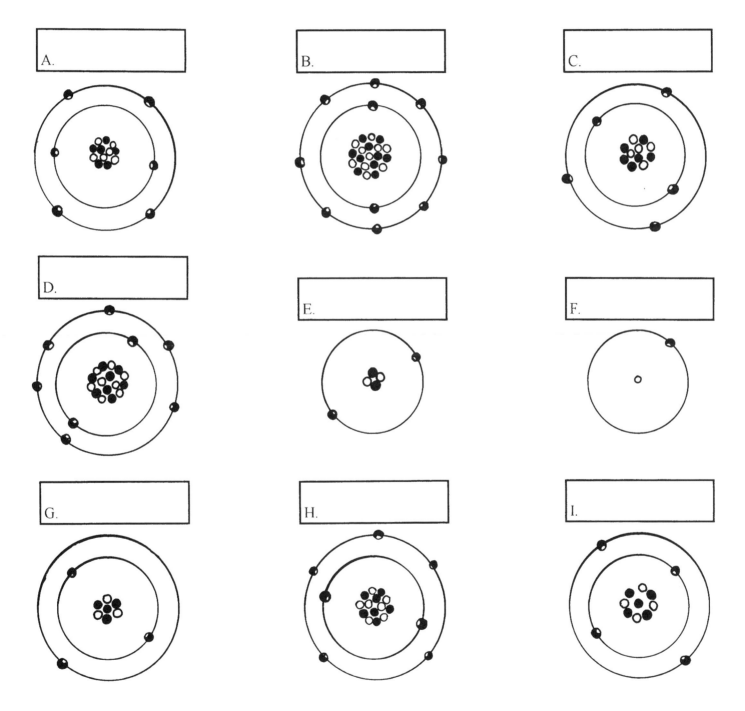

A.

B.

C.

D.

E.

F.

G.

H.

I.

Name _____

A WORLD-FAMOUS TABLE

There is a table (not one for dinner) that's probably the most famous table of science. (You can find it in your physical science book or on page 52 of this book.) If you learn how to read it, you'll have quick access to important stuff about elements. It's called the Periodic Table (because it's written in rows, called periods). Build your skill at reading the Periodic Table by finding the missing information in the samples below. You can get more practice with the Periodic Table on pages 11, 13, 14, and 15 of this book.

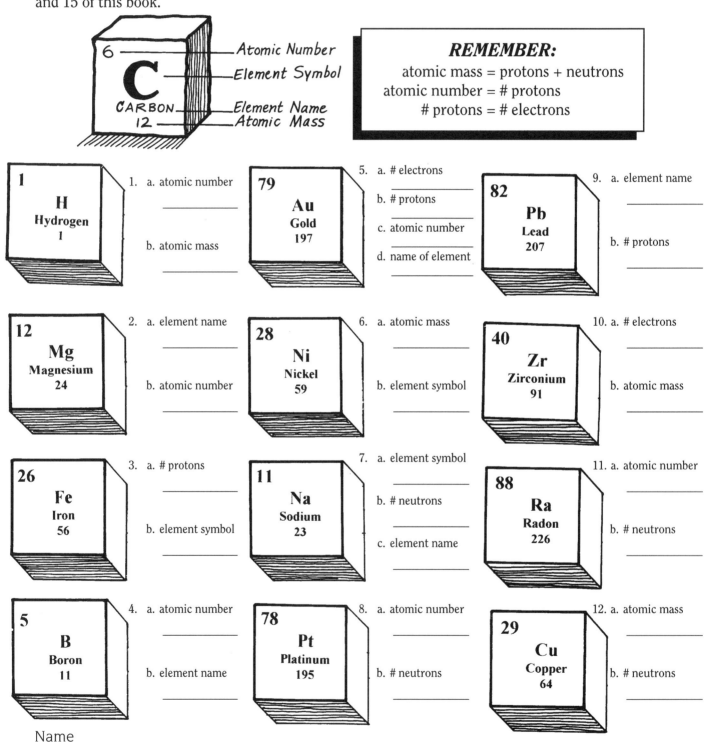

REMEMBER:
atomic mass = protons + neutrons
atomic number = # protons
protons = # electrons

1. a. atomic number
   _____
   b. atomic mass
   _____

2. a. element name
   _____
   b. atomic number
   _____

3. a. # protons
   _____
   b. element symbol
   _____

4. a. atomic number
   _____
   b. element name
   _____

5. a. # electrons
   _____
   b. # protons
   _____
   c. atomic number
   _____
   d. name of element
   _____

6. a. atomic mass
   _____
   b. element symbol
   _____

7. a. element symbol
   _____
   b. # neutrons
   _____
   c. element name
   _____

8. a. atomic number
   _____
   b. # neutrons
   _____

9. a. element name
   _____
   b. # protons
   _____

10. a. # electrons
    _____
    b. atomic mass
    _____

11. a. atomic number
    _____
    b. # neutrons
    _____

12. a. atomic mass
    _____
    b. # neutrons
    _____

Name _____

Basic Skills/Physical Science 6-8+

WHO AM I?

These mystery elements are waiting to be identified. The trick is—you'll need the Periodic Table to unmask their identities. Unless you have it memorized, you'll need a copy of the table from your science book or from page 52 of this book. Read the clues about each mystery element, figure out what it is, and then write the name and symbol of the element.

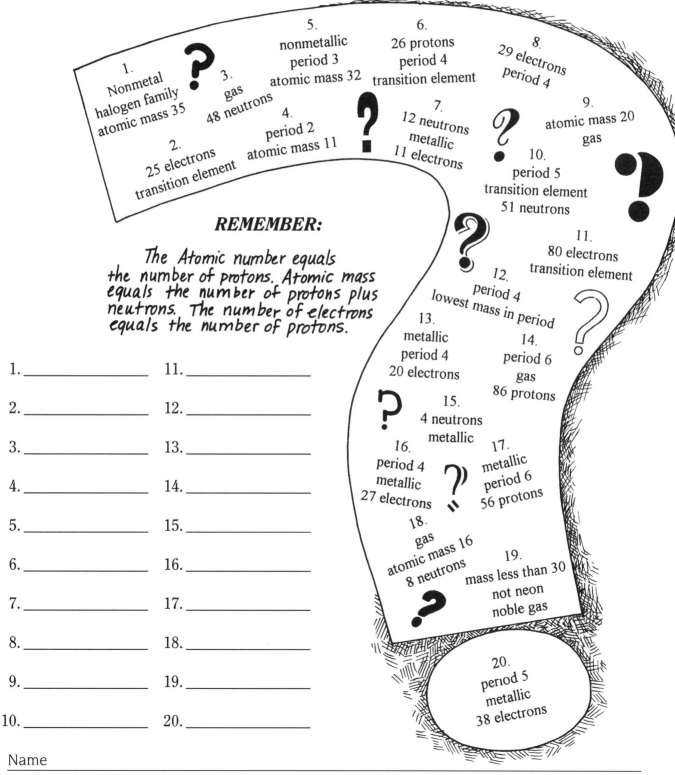

1.
Nonmetal
halogen family
atomic mass 35

2.
25 electrons
transition element

3.
gas
48 neutrons

4.
period 2
atomic mass 11

5.
nonmetallic
period 3
atomic mass 32

6.
26 protons
period 4
transition element

7.
12 neutrons
metallic
11 electrons

8.
29 electrons
period 4

9.
atomic mass 20
gas

10.
period 5
transition element
51 neutrons

11.
80 electrons
transition element

12.
period 4
lowest mass in period

13.
metallic
period 4
20 electrons

14.
period 6
gas
86 protons

15.
4 neutrons
metallic

16.
period 4
metallic
27 electrons

17.
metallic
period 6
56 protons

18.
gas
atomic mass 16
8 neutrons

19.
mass less than 30
not neon
noble gas

20.
period 5
metallic
38 electrons

REMEMBER:

The Atomic number equals the number of protons. Atomic mass equals the number of protons plus neutrons. The number of electrons equals the number of protons.

1. _____   11. _____

2. _____   12. _____

3. _____   13. _____

4. _____   14. _____

5. _____   15. _____

6. _____   16. _____

7. _____   17. _____

8. _____   18. _____

9. _____   19. _____

10. _____   20. _____

Name _____

QUARKS, ISOTOPES, & OTHER CURIOSITIES

Atoms and elements have all kinds of interesting properties and "quirks." One of them is even called a "quark." If you don't know how to answer these questions already from your study of physical science, keep a science book, encyclopedia, or other references handy to help you identify the curiosities of elements and atoms. (See the Periodic Table on page 52 of this book.)

1. Does a neutron have an electric charge? _____

2. What charge does a proton have? _____

3. What charge does an electron have? _____

4. What is the electron cloud of an atom? _____

5. What are the "energy levels" of the electron cloud? _____

6. Which energy level holds no more than 8 electrons? _____

7. Can there be 4 electrons in the first energy level? _____

8. Can there be 20 electrons in the third energy level? _____

9. How many electrons can there be in a level beyond the third? _____

10. If an atom has 16 electrons, how many are in the third level? _____

11. If an atom has 26 electrons, what is the least number of energy levels it has? _____

12. What is an isotope? _____

13. If a hydrogen atom has 2 neutrons, is it an isotope? _____

14. If a hydrogen atom has a mass of 3, is it an isotope? _____

15. What is a quark? _____

CHARGES

POSITIVE

NEGATIVE

NEUTRAL

ENERGY LEVELS

ELECTRON CLOUDS

QUARKS

ISOTOPES

Complete the chart below. Fill in the number of electrons in each energy level.

Element	Total	Level 1	Level 2	Level 3
A. Carbon				
B. Mercury				
C. Calcium				
D. Krypton				
E. Neon				
F. Arsenic				
G. Sodium				

Name _____

ELEMENTARY FACTS

Get to know common elements a little better by tracking down the facts that match these clues. They're lurking around the edges of the page; you just have to figure out which one belongs where.

mercury

allotrope

carbon

aluminum

iron

silicon

properties

ore

alkali

organic

metals

1. vertical columns in the Periodic Table
2. elements in families have similar _____
3. family of "salt-producing" elements
4. family in Group 18 on Periodic Table
5. horizontal rows on Periodic Table
6. each element in a period is in a _____ group
7. elements on left side of Periodic Table
8. elements on right side of Periodic Table
9. elements in Groups 3–12 on Periodic Table
10. number of electrons transition elements have in outer energy level
11. most reactive metals
12. most widely used metal
13. only metal liquid at room temperature
14. natural material from which metals can be profitably extracted
15. formed by metals; contains more than one element and has metallic properties
16. most abundant element in Earth's crust
17. odorless, tasteless, colorless gas; lightest of all elements
18. different form of same element due to different arrangements of atoms
19. second most abundant element in Earth's crust; found in glass and sand
20. gas element safe to use in balloons
21. compounds that contain carbon
22. element contained in 80% of known compounds

different

noble gas

families

two

halogen

hydrogen

periods

transition

helium

nonmetals

alloy

Name

SIMPLY SYMBOLS

How sharp is your knowledge of the symbols for elements? This puzzle is already solved, using symbols of common elements. The clues (names of the elements) are missing. See how many you can name without looking for help in any resources. Write the element name next to the matching puzzle number.

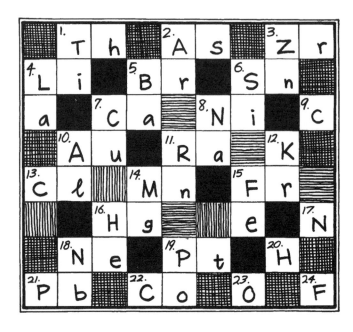

Down

1. _____
2. _____
3. _____
4. _____
5. _____
6. _____
7. _____
8. _____
10. _____
11. _____
12. _____
14. _____
15. _____
16. _____
18. _____
19. _____

Across

1. _____
2. _____
3. _____
4. _____
5. _____
6. _____
7. _____
8. _____
9. _____
10. _____
11. _____
12. _____
13. _____
14. _____

15. _____
16. _____
17. _____
18. _____
19. _____
20. _____
21. _____
22. _____
23. _____
24. _____

Name _____

A MATTER OF MATTER

You're surrounded! Everything around you is matter because matter is anything that has mass and takes up space. You've learned about the three ordinary states of matter. The difference between these states has to do with how tightly particles are packed together and how they move.

I. Name and describe the three ordinary forms of matter below. Label each circle with its form. Then write a description of the characteristics of each state, and tell something about the motion of the molecules.

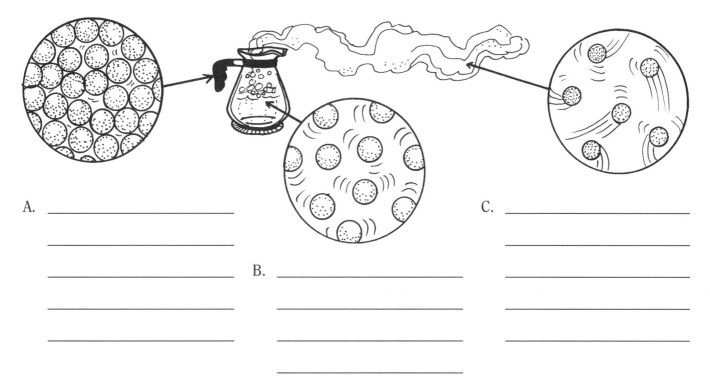

A. _____

_____

_____

_____

_____

B. _____

_____

_____

_____

C. _____

_____

_____

_____

II. Match these rules about matter with their meanings.

_____ 1. Boyle's Law

_____ 2. Charles' Law

_____ 3. Archimedes' Principle

_____ 4. Pascal's Principle

_____ 5. Bernoulli's Principle

A. The amount of force a fluid (liquid or gas) uses to push up an object that's been placed in it is equal to the weight of the fluid that was pushed out of the way by the object.

B. When you decrease the size of the container that a gas is in, the gas will exert more pressure on the container.

C. Pressure put on a fluid stays the same throughout the fluid.

D. As long as you don't change the pressure of a sample of gas, the volume of the gas will increase as the temperature rises.

E. Pressure in a fluid is high where the velocity is low and low where the velocity is high.

III. Describe the fourth state of matter (use the back of this sheet or another sheet of paper).

Name _____

MOLECULES ON THE MOVE

There's something that gets molecules in matter moving (or slows their movement) enough to cause changes in states of matter. That "something" is heat—or the absence of it! The state of matter depends on temperature. When temperatures go up or down enough, almost all matter will change.

Show that you understand how temperature changes states of matter by writing an explanation of what happens to cause each of these events below.

1. The punch you poured in the ice cube trays last night is a supply of popsicles today.
    _____
    _____
    _____

4. The big ice cubes you put in your water are now tiny.
    _____
    _____
    _____

7. The wet sponge you left on the counter last night is dry this morning.
    _____
    _____
    _____

2. You forgot to turn off the teakettle, and now the water is gone.
    _____
    _____
    _____

5. The chicken soup has boiled for half an hour and it seems to have "shrunk."
    _____
    _____
    _____

8. Your little brother is crying because his snowman is shrinking. _____
    _____
    _____
    _____

3. The cold, hard butter you spread on your toast is now soft and runny. _____
    _____
    _____
    _____

6. When you put the lid on the simmering soup, the inside of the lid gets all wet. _____
    _____
    _____
    _____

9. Your mom hung your jeans outside on the clothesline, the temperature dropped below freezing, and your jeans are cold, hard, and stiff.
    _____
    _____
    _____
    _____

Name _____

THE TRUTH OF THE MATTER

Do these scientists know their stuff? They've made a list of "true" statements about some matters of matter. Are all their "pronouncements" really true? Write **T** for the true ones. For erroneous statements, make corrections needed to clear up the errors.

_____ 1. Volume is the amount of space a substance of matter occupies.

_____ 2. Mass and weight of matter are the same thing.

_____ 3. You find the density of a substance by dividing its volume by its weight.

_____ 4. All matter has mass.

_____ 5. In a mixture, elements or compounds are blended without a chemical reaction.

_____ 6. Compounds are chemically bonded together.

_____ 7. A colloid has smaller particles than a solution.

_____ 8. In a suspension, particles cannot be seen through a microscope.

_____ 9. Butter, toothpaste, paint, whipped cream, and fog are all colloids.

I HAVE THE SOLUTION !

_____ 10. Not all matter takes up space.

_____ 11. A boiling point is a chemical property of a substance.

_____ 12. In a homogeneous mixture, particles are spread evenly throughout the mixture.

_____ 13. The ability of metals to rust is a physical property of metals.

_____ 14. The speed of evaporation is a physical property of a liquid.

_____ 15. The density of a substance is a physical property.

_____ 16. Sublimation is the change from a solid to a gas without becoming a liquid first.

_____ 17. Viscosity is a property of a gas.

_____ 18. A solution is a kind of a mixture.

Name _____

GREAT COMBINATIONS

Most of the solids, liquids, and gases around you exist because of their ability to combine, or chemically bond, with other elements and make new substances—called compounds. All compounds are created by chemical reactions in which the atoms rearrange themselves and share particles. Once atoms decide to bond, they often hang on tightly to their new arrangement and are not easy to split apart. Each of these groupings of atoms on this page and the next (page 21) shows the atoms that would make up one molecule of a compound. The compound is named, and the atoms are pictured. It's your job to write the formula that shows the makeup of the compound.

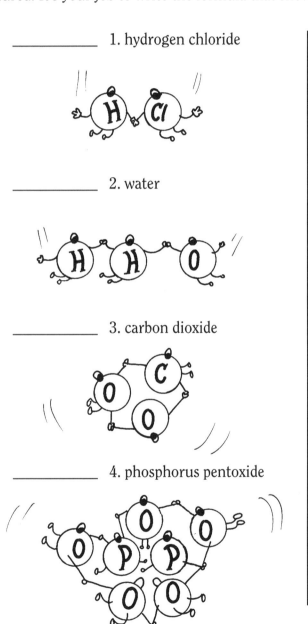

_____ 1. hydrogen chloride

_____ 2. water

_____ 3. carbon dioxide

_____ 4. phosphorus pentoxide

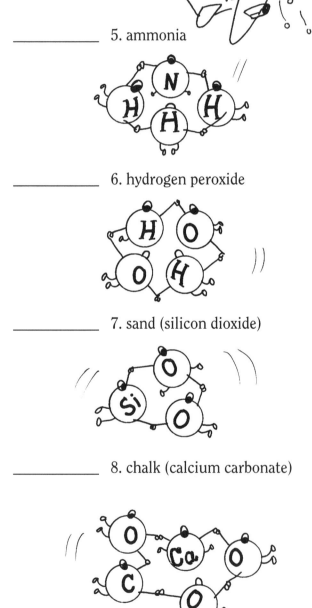

_____ 5. ammonia

_____ 6. hydrogen peroxide

_____ 7. sand (silicon dioxide)

_____ 8. chalk (calcium carbonate)

Use with page 21.

Name _____

GREAT COMBINATIONS, CONTINUED

Use with page 20.
Write the chemical formula for each compound.

_____ 9. baking soda (sodium hydrogen carbonate)

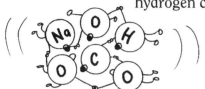

_____ 10. silver nitrate

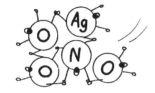

_____ 11. methane

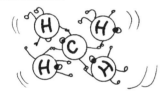

_____ 12. sodium peroxide

_____ 13. carbon monoxide

_____ 14. nitrogen dioxide

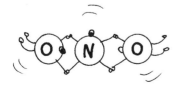

_____ 15. lead monoxide

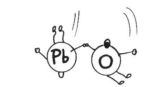

_____ 16. sulfuric acid

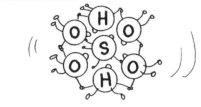

_____ 17. hydrogen bromide

_____ 18. hydrogen fluoride

_____ 19. silver chloride

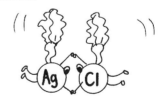

_____ 20. salt (sodium chloride)

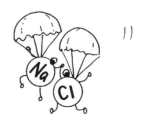

Name _____

21

TWO WAYS TO CHANGE

A melting ice sculpture . . . a spectacular bonfire . . . a cake baking in the oven . . . a milkshake in the making . . . an explosion . . . all of these involve changes in matter. Some are physical changes (changes in shape, color, or state) and others are chemical changes (changes involving chemical reactions). Which are which? For each change described below, write **P** for physical change or **C** for chemical change. Be ready to explain your choices.

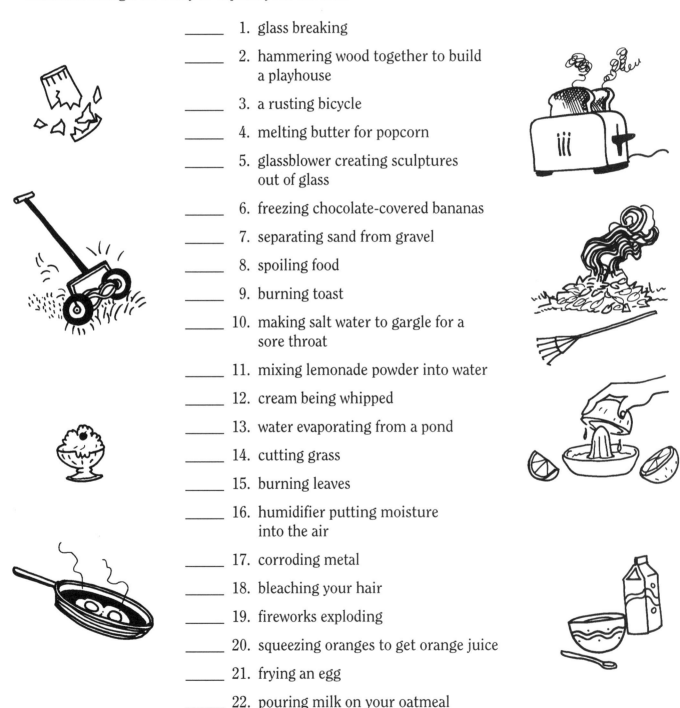

_____ 1. glass breaking

_____ 2. hammering wood together to build a playhouse

_____ 3. a rusting bicycle

_____ 4. melting butter for popcorn

_____ 5. glassblower creating sculptures out of glass

_____ 6. freezing chocolate-covered bananas

_____ 7. separating sand from gravel

_____ 8. spoiling food

_____ 9. burning toast

_____ 10. making salt water to gargle for a sore throat

_____ 11. mixing lemonade powder into water

_____ 12. cream being whipped

_____ 13. water evaporating from a pond

_____ 14. cutting grass

_____ 15. burning leaves

_____ 16. humidifier putting moisture into the air

_____ 17. corroding metal

_____ 18. bleaching your hair

_____ 19. fireworks exploding

_____ 20. squeezing oranges to get orange juice

_____ 21. frying an egg

_____ 22. pouring milk on your oatmeal

Name _____

COMPOUNDS WITH CHARACTER

There are hundreds of compounds that are "interesting characters!" Some of them are organic—meaning they contain carbon and often are only found in living organisms. Others are inorganic. They contain no carbon and are not living, but are fascinating and useful just the same. These clues describe some interesting characteristics of a few organic and inorganic compounds. Match the right clue with the right answer. (An answer may be used more than once.)

HYDROGEN

NEUTRALIZATION

alkali(s)

carbon dioxide

enzyme

vitamins

CARBOHYDRATE

sugar

unsaturated

amino acids

base(s)

acid(s)

starch

POLYMER

PHENOLPHTHALEIN

lipids

proteins

HYDROCARBON

saturated

pH

isomers

CLUES

_____ 1. given off when acids react with metals

_____ 2. chemical opposite of an acid

_____ 3. giant organic molecule made of small molecules linked together

_____ 4. compound that produces hydronium ions in water

_____ 5. ants, vinegar, lemons, car batteries

_____ 6. compounds commonly known as fats and oils

_____ 7. soapy

_____ 8. a protein that speeds up chemical reactions in living systems

_____ 9. group of polymers contained by all living organisms

_____ 10. produced when acids react with carbonates

_____ 11. deodorant, baking soda, oven cleaner, antacid tablets

_____ 12. organic molecule that has hydrogen and oxygen present in a 2(H) to 1(O) ratio

_____ 13. scale for measuring acidity

_____ 14. compounds with the same molecular formula but different structures

_____ 15. chemical opposite of a base

_____ 16. will soothe an acid stomach

_____ 17. compound that contains only hydrogen and carbon

_____ 18. an indicator for detecting an acid or base

_____ 19. examples of carbohydrates

_____ 20. turns blue litmus red

_____ 21. classes of organic compounds

_____ 22. hydrocarbons with one or more double or triple bonds

_____ 23. hydrocarbons with single bonds between C and H atoms

_____ 24. happens when an acid is added to a base

_____ 25. inorganic compounds that cells use for chemical changes in the body

Name _____

CHEMISTRY CHALLENGE

Take the challenge to win $10,000! Do it by writing the question for every answer on the game board. Questions get harder as the value increases. You win the first amount for a correct answer, but you lose the second amount for each wrong answer. A correct answer for each BONUS square doubles your winnings for that square. (A wrong answer doubles the loss.) Write each answer, in the form of a question, on the answer form on page 26. When you've mastered this challenge, go on to the DOUBLE CHEMISTRY CHALLENGE on page 25. Correct answers on both pages can win $30,000!

MATTER

1. The three states of matter
$100 (-$50)

2. BONUS
Matter that has no definite shape or volume
$200 (-$100)

3. Matter that has a definite volume but no definite shape
$300 (-$150)

4. Matter in which molecules are packed tightly together and move only slightly
$400 (-$200)

5. Repeating pattern arrangement of particles in most solids
$500 (-$250)

6. Property of liquid that describes how it pours
$600 (-$300)

ELEMENTS

7. Smallest particle of an element that has all the properties of that element
$100 (-$50)

8. Equal to the number or protons in an atom; found on Periodic Table
$200 (-$100)

9. Region around the nucleus of an atom occupied by electrons
$300 (-$150)

10. Elements with 5 or more electrons in the outer energy level
$400 (-$200)

11. The simplest element
$500 (-$250)

12. BONUS
Elements with 1-2 electrons in the outer energy level
$600 (-$300)

COMPOUNDS

13. Kind of change during which compounds are formed
$100 (-$50)

14. Group of symbols that represent a compound
$200 (-$100)

15. BONUS
Formed when 2 or more atoms bond by sharing electrons
$300 (-$150)

16. Charged particle resulting when an atom loses one or more electrons
$400 (-$200)

17. A common compound with 2 hydrogen and 2 oxygen atoms
$500 (-$250)

18. The chemical formula for magnesium chloride
$600 (-$300)

PHYSICAL CHANGES

19. Point at which matter changes from a solid to a liquid
$100 (-$50)

20. Point at which a liquid changes to a gas
$200 (-$100)

21. Point at which a liquid changes to a solid
$300 (-$150)

22. A change of matter from vapor to liquid
$400 (-$200)

23. BONUS
A change of matter from liquid to gas without boiling
$500 (-$250)

24. Factor that usually contributes to physical change in the state of matter
$600 (-$300)

Take the Chemistry Challenge and win big! Score points by writing the correct question for each answer on the game board. Watch out! The higher you score, the harder the questions become! A BONUS earns double value for a correct question, but you risk losing double as well. So, bone up on your Chemistry trivia.

Name

DOUBLE CHEMISTRY CHALLENGE

Take this challenge to win $20,000! Do it by writing the correct question for every answer on the game board. Questions get harder as the value increases. You win the first amount for a correct answer, but you lose the second amount for each wrong answer. A correct answer for each BONUS square doubles your winnings for that square. (A wrong answer doubles the loss.) Write each answer, in the form of a question, on the answer form on page 26. If you combine this with the CHEMISTRY CHALLENGE on page 24, you can win up to $30,000!

MIXTURES & SOLUTIONS	CHEMICAL REACTIONS	ORGANIC CHEMISTRY	ACIDS, BASES, & SALTS
1. Substance in which a solute is dissolved $200 (-$100)	**7.** A factor that speeds up a chemical reaction $200 (-$100)	**13.** Element found in all organic compounds $200 (-$100)	**19.** Substance that produces hydrogen ions in water $200 (-$100)
2. The amount of solute that can be dissolved in an amount of solvent $400 (-$200)	**8.** BONUS Released or absorbed in a chemical change $400 (-$200)	**14.** Compounds that contain only carbon and hydrogen atoms $400 (-$200)	**20.** Blue or red indicator used to test for acids or bases $400 (-$200)
3. When all the solute a solution can hold is dissolved $600 (-$300)	**9.** A factor that slows down a chemical reaction $600 (-$300)	**15.** Compounds with the same molecular formula but different structures $600 (-$300)	**21.** BONUS Measure of acidity in terms of hydronium ion concentration $600 (-$300)
4. Mixture in which substances are not spread out evenly $800 (-$400)	**10.** Shows changes that take place during a chemical reaction $800 (-$400)	**16.** Giant molecule made of many small organic molecules linked together $800 (-$400)	**22.** Common household base compound formed from nitrogen and hydrogen $800 (-$400)
5. An insoluble solid in a liquid $1000 (-$500)	**11.** An insoluble substance that crystallizes out of solution $1000 (-$500)	**17.** BONUS Organic molecules with ratio of 2 hydrogen atoms to one oxygen atom $1000 (-$500)	**23.** Strong base commonly known as lye $1000 (-$500)
6. BONUS A way of separating 2 liquids which have different boiling points $1200 (-$600)	**12.** Reaction that combines 2 or more substances into a new compound $1200 (-$600)	**18.** Organic compound with carboxylic acid group and amino group $1200 (-$600)	**24.** Formed from a positive ion from a base and a negative ion from an acid $1200 (-$600)

Name

Basic Skills/Physical Science 6-8+

SCORE SHEET FOR CHEMISTRY CHALLENGES

Use with pages 24 and 25.
*—Bonus; doubles value

MATTER	Score
$100	
*$200	
$300	
$400	
$500	
$600	

MIXTURES & SOLUTIONS	Score
$200	
$400	
$600	
$800	
$1000	
*$1200	

ELEMENTS	Score
$100	
$200	
$300	
$400	
$500	
*$600	

CHEMICAL REACTIONS	Score
$200	
*$400	
$600	
$800	
$1000	
$1200	

COMPOUNDS	Score
$100	
$200	
*$300	
$400	
$500	
$600	

ORGANIC CHEMISTRY	Score
$200	
$400	
$600	
$800	
*$1000	
$1200	

PHYSICAL CHANGES	Score
$100	
$200	
$300	
$400	
*$500	
$600	

ACIDS, BASES, & SALTS	Score
$200	
$400	
*$600	
$800	
$1000	
$1200	

TOTAL SCORE _____   TOTAL SCORE _____

TOTAL CHALLENGE & DOUBLE CHALLENGE SCORE _____
Possible Winnings: $30,000

You can play this game with a group, too. You'll need to make up new rules, new scoring directions, and whatever you need to make it a fun, challenging game.

Name _____

NOTIONS ABOUT MOTIONS

Skydivers leaping out of an airplane, kids doing tricks on skateboards, rollercoasters circling in upside-down loops, commuters riding on subways, people dancing—motion is all around us. In order to describe a motion, you have to know where the object begins. The beginning position (the skydiver in the airplane) is the reference point from which you can describe the distance moved (200 feet into a freefall). Many other terms are used to describe aspects of motion. Many of them are scrambled below. Find the scrambled term that matches each clue. Then unscramble it, and write it next to the clue.

yolevict   deeps   tear   talicecerona

trainie   noctrifi   ster   smas   snotnew

tommemun   nertlaim   ira traicnesse

tridenioc   spira   noholzatir   clatrive

lateptricne   crofe

vragyti   sperruse

_____ 1. the rate of change in velocity

_____ 2. describes the speed and direction of an object

_____ 3. the amount of an object

_____ 4. the greatest velocity a falling object reaches

_____ 5. velocity parallel to Earth's surface

_____ 6. the force on an object pulling toward the center of a circular path

_____ 7. the rate of change in position (or rate of motion)

_____ 8. ratio between two different quantities

_____ 9. property of a body that resists any change in velocity

_____ 10. zero velocity

_____ 11. mass of an object multiplied by its velocity

_____ 12. upward force of air against a moving object

_____ 13. velocity in an up or down direction

_____ 14. unit of measurement for force

_____ 15. a push or pull exerted on one body by another

_____ 16. Forces always come in _____ .

_____ 17. Two objects with the same velocity must be moving in the same _____ .

_____ 18. a force that acts on all objects on Earth

_____ 19. the force that opposes the motion of two touching surfaces

_____ 20. amount of force per unit area

Name _____

WHICH LAW?

We're told that Sir Isaac Newton discovered some things about motion when an apple dropped on his head. Whatever "force" was behind his discoveries, we have benefited from his discoveries.
Here are his three laws of motion. You should be familiar with them. Fill in the missing words in each of the three laws. Then tell which law fits each example below.

Which law? First, Second, or Third?

_____ 1. A frog leaping upward off his lily pad is pulled downward by gravity and lands on another lily pad instead of continuing on in a straight line.

_____ 2. As the fuel in a rocket ignites, the force of the gas expansion and explosion pushes out the back of the rocket and pushes the rocket forward.

_____ 3. When you are standing up in a subway train, and the train suddenly stops, your body continues to go forward.

_____ 4. After you start up your motorbike, as you give it more gas, it goes faster.

_____ 5. A pitched baseball goes faster than one that is gently thrown.

_____ 6. A swimmer pushes water back with her arms, but her body moves forward.

_____ 7. As an ice skater pushes harder with his leg muscles, he begins to move faster.

_____ 8. When Bobby, age 5, and his dad are skipping pebbles on the pond, the pebbles that Bobby's dad throws go farther and faster than his.

_____ 9. When you paddle a canoe, the canoe goes forward.

_____ 10. A little girl who has been pulling a sled behind her in the snow is crying because when she stopped to tie her hat on, the sled kept moving and hit her in the back of her legs.

NEWTON'S FIRST LAW OF MOTION:
An object at _____ stays at _____ or an object that is _____ at a _____ in a straight _____ keeps moving at that _____ unless another _____ acts on it.

NEWTON'S SECOND LAW OF MOTION:
The amount of _____ needed to make an object change its _____ depends on the _____ of the object and the _____ required.

NEWTON'S THIRD LAW OF MOTION:
For every _____ (or force), there is an _____ and _____ action (or force).

Name _____

WHAT'S YOUR MOTION IQ?

Do you know the difference between velocity and inertia? . . . acceleration and rate? . . . speed and velocity? . . . gravity and centripetal force? . . . momentum and inertia? . . . friction and air resistance? If you have those all straight, you'll be able to tell which is operating in each of these examples. Choose from the list of terms. A term may be used more than once.

1. A car hits a tree and doesn't stop, but keeps going until it's severely damaged. Why? _____

2. When a space capsule returns to Earth after a mission, it glows red-hot as it enters the atmosphere because of _____ .

3. Mark and his friends love the Terminator roller coaster because of its two 360° loops. Nobody falls out when the cars are upside-down because of _____ .

rate
distance
inertia
centripetal force
gravity
friction
velocity
acceleration
air resistance
momentum

AND AWAY WE GO!

4. Josh and Ramon head toward each other on their rollerblades at the same, breakneck speed. But, because they are going opposite directions, they do not share the same _____ .

5. The blade of an ice skate melts the ice beneath it and reduces _____ .

6. Joleen shoots an arrow at a target many feet away, but the arrow curves toward the ground before it gets to the target, due to the force of _____ .

7. The sleek shape of a bobsled reduces _____ and allows greater speeds.

8. A pool player hits the eight ball which slams into a second ball. The eight ball stops, but the second ball goes forward, because of _____ .

9. Michael waxes his skis so they'll go faster. He's reducing the force of _____ .

10. Scott falls off his skateboard. He comes to a crashing stop against the sidewalk, but his skateboard rolls on because of _____ .

11. Showing off, Megan swings a bucket of water around in circles, upside-down. No water spills out. Why?_____

12. The snowboard sits at the bottom of the hill, unmoving, until Andrea gets on it and pushes it along. _____ kept it from moving.

13. Jim's little sister isn't swinging very high, so he gives her a huge push to get her higher. This shows an increase in _____ .

14. Kate drops her math paper out of her second floor bedroom window to share with her friend, Evan, who is waiting below. It takes a really long time for the paper to get down to him because of _____ .

15. Tom bragged to Tara that he watched a centipede crawl the whole length of his room in the time he did his homework. His room is 16 feet long and his homework took 2.5 hours, so he's saying the centipede traveled at 6.4 feet per hour. What characteristic of motion has he calculated?_____

Name

PROBLEMS WITH TRAINS

What is it about trains that makes them so popular in problems about motion? Well, probably it's the fact that it's usually speeding along or chugging along in a steady motion—going somewhere beyond wherever you are. In keeping with the tradition of train problems, practice your calculations with rate of motion by solving these questions.

REMEMBER:

Distance = rate x time

SO: Time = distance ÷ rate

AND: Rate = distance ÷ time

1. The *Midnight Express* heading west from Chicago to Albuquerque travels at 100 mph for 160 miles. How much time does this take?

2. A train that's heading west leaves a station at the same time that an eastbound train 840 miles away leaves its station. They both travel at an average speed of 120 mph. How long will it take before they meet?

3. If the *West Coast Skyliner* is traveling north at 120 mph and the *Skyliner II* is traveling south at 120 mph, do these trains have the same speed? Do they have the same velocity?

4. The *Black Giant* heads west for 16 hours traveling at an average speed of 120 mph. The *Speed Demon* leaves the same station and heads west on a parallel track, traveling at 95 mph for 20 hours. After these amounts of time, which train will have covered more distance?

5. Two trains leave their stations, which are 2860 miles apart, at the same time—8:00 A.M. central time. They both travel at 110 mph toward each other on the same track. At what time (central time) will they meet?

6. The *Rocky Mountain Cruiser* covers 3105 miles in 27 hours. What is its rate?

7. You are on a train that is going east at 95 mph. You are walking at 5 mph toward the front of the train. In relation to the passengers seated on the train, how fast are you moving?

8. In the same situation above, how fast are you moving in relation to the kid standing beside the railroad track, watching the train go by?

9. The *Appalachian Express* and the *Mississippi Streamer,* starting 2184 miles apart, leave at the same time, heading toward each other. They meet in 12 hours. The *Appalachian Express* has traveled at a rate of 85 mph, and the *Mississippi Streamer* has traveled at a rate of 97 mph. How far has the *Mississippi Streamer* traveled when they meet?

10. The *Quebec Racer* travels for 6 hours at 105 mph. The *Chicago Skyscraper* travels for 8.5 hours at 92 mph. Which train covers more distance? How much more?

Name

THE HEAT IS ON

You reach out to stir the soup and the spoon burns your hand. Your can of soda was icy cold just half an hour ago, but now it's lukewarm. The basement of your house is cool, even on a sweltering hot day. You're sweating in your black shirt on a sunny day, but your friend is comfortable in her white shirt. You ski outside all day on a sub-zero, blizzardy day. You're warm in your living room even though you're 20 feet across the room from the heater. All these things are true because of the amazing talent of heat energy (it can be transferred) and the equally amazing talents of some materials that put up resistance to heat transfer. Use your knowledge about heat energy to do these two tasks:

I. Fill in the diagram below, and write a brief explanation for each method. Be sure to mention what kind of material (metal, wood, water, air, etc.) that method works in.

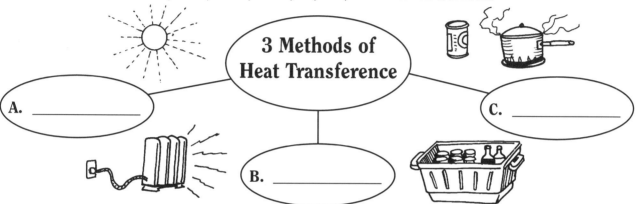

II. Give explanations that answer these questions. Use the back of the page if you need to.

1. How does heat get from the stove burner into your soup?
2. How does a cooler keep drinks cold on a hot day?
3. When two cars sit in the sun all day, the one with the black roof gets hotter than the one with the white, shiny roof. Why?
4. How does the heat from the sun, thousands of miles away, reach your body?
5. Why is the metal spoon in your cup of hot chocolate hot?
6. Why doesn't a plastic spoon in hot chocolate feel hot?
7. Why is your house warm on a cold day, even if you haven't turned on the heat?
8. When you turn on a heater, how does the warmth get to you?
9. Why are you warmer with several layers of clothes than with one heavy jacket?
10. Why do some cooking pots have wooden handles?
11. How does a cold can of soda become warm on a hot day?
12. How does a microwave oven get your food hot?
13. How can a solar heating system heat your water on a day when there's no sun?
14. How is a refrigerator an example of a heat mover?
15. How can temperature (heat) be pollution?
16. Why does clean snow melt more slowly than dirty snow?
17. Why is the attic of a house always warmer than the basement?

Name

SOME FORCEFUL LESSONS

Forces and energy—they're all around you! They keep your feet from slipping out from underneath you. They keep the moon from flying off into space. They make your favorite sports activities possible. They keep the drink in your glass from floating up into your face. They provide the thrills you get at an amusement park or on a water slide.

Make the correct choices about the kinds of forces or energy in these examples. Circle each right answer.

1. What keeps your feet from sliding out from underneath you with every step you take?

   (friction, gravity, work)

2. Why do your hands get warm when you rub them together?

   (potential energy, centripetal force, friction)

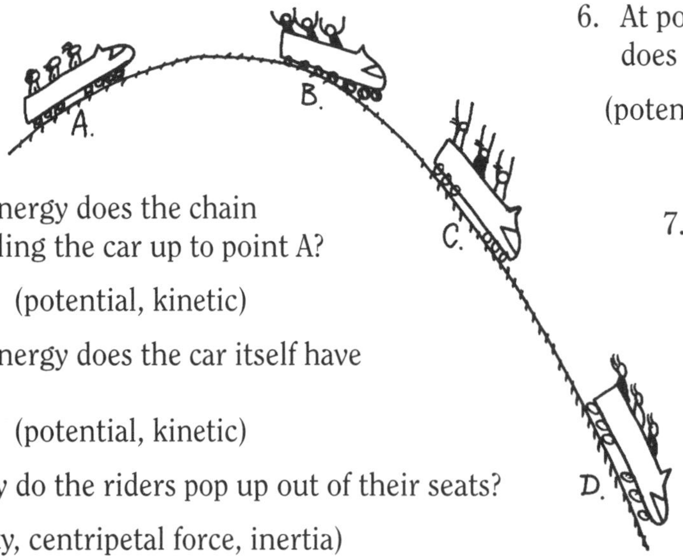

6. At point C, what kind of energy does the car have?

   (potential, mechanical, kinetic)

3. What kind of energy does the chain have that's pulling the car up to point A?

   (potential, kinetic)

7. At point D, what force is pulling the car down hill?

   (friction, gravity, centripetal)

4. What kind of energy does the car itself have at point A?

   (potential, kinetic)

5. At point B, why do the riders pop up out of their seats?

   (gravity, centripetal force, inertia)

8. What kind of energy is shown in X, when the boy is pushing by bending back his legs?

   (kinetic, potential)

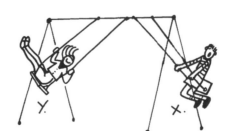

9. What kind of energy is shown in Y, when the girl's legs are extended?

   (potential, kinetic)

Use with page 33.

Name

SOME FORCEFUL LESSONS, CONTINUED

Use with page 32.

P

Q

10. What kind of energy is represented by the gasoline pump?

(potential, kinetic)

11. What kind of energy is shown in P? (mechanical, potential, kinetic)

12. What kind of energy is shown in Q? (mechanical, potential, kinetic)

13. What type of energy is shown here?

(potential, kinetic)

15. What kinds of energy are represented here? (mechanical, potential, kinetic)

16. What type of energy is shown here?

(thermal, mechanical)

14. What kind of energy is represented by the food being eaten? (mechanical, potential, kinetic)

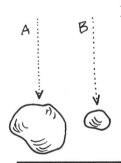

A   B

17. Which will reach the ground first, A or B? _____ Why? _____

_____

_____

_____

A   B

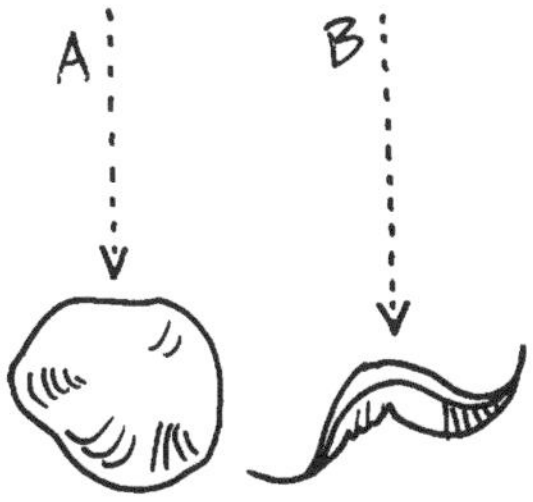

18. Which will reach the ground first, A or B? _____ Why? _____

_____

_____

_____

19. Where will this astro-naut weigh the most? (moon, Earth) Why? _____

_____

_____

_____

20. How much difference is there between the astronaut's mass on Earth and on the moon?

_____

_____

_____

Name

SIMPLE, BUT TOUGH

When you think of machines, you probably think of complex modern machines such as computers, elaborate stereo systems, cars, robots, or spaceships. Actually, machines are not a modern invention. They've been around for thousands of years. And all of them, even the modern ones, are either simple machines or combinations of simple machines.

I. Define these:

A. work _____

_____

B. machine _____

_____

C. simple machine _____

_____

D. mechanical advantage _____

_____

E. resistance force _____

_____

F. effort force _____

_____

II. Name each machine, and tell how it makes work simpler.

1. _____

_____

_____

_____

2. _____

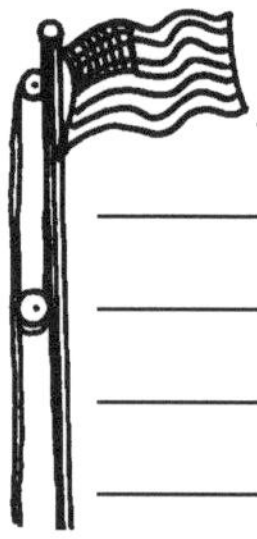

_____

_____

3. _____

_____

_____

_____

4. _____

_____

_____

_____

5. _____

_____

_____

_____

6. _____

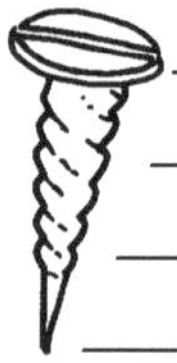

_____

_____

_____

Use with page 35.

Name _____

SIMPLE, BUT TOUGH, CONTINUED

Use with page 34.

III. Tell what simple machine is represented by each picture.

1. _____ 2. _____ 3. _____ 4. _____

5. _____ 6. _____ 7. _____ 8. _____

9. _____ 10. _____ 11. _____ 12. _____

13. _____ 14. _____ 15. _____ 16. _____

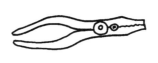

17. _____ 18. _____ 19. _____ 20. _____

Name _____

Basic Skills/Physical Science 6-8+

PROFILE OF A WAVE

Sound waves, water waves, radio waves, microwaves, electromagnetic waves, light waves, X-rays, gamma rays, and more! These are some (but not all) of the different kinds of waves traveling in the world. A wave is a rhythmic disturbance that carries energy from one place to another. The many different kinds of waves share many characteristics. Some of them are shown on this wave that's being made by kids shaking a rope up and down. Answer the following questions about wave characteristics.

1. What is the distance called that is represented by the arrow Z?_____

2. What letter is labeling the wave's trough?_____

3. What letter is labeling a wave's crest?_____

4. The number of waves that pass the poster per second is called the _____ of the waves.

5. If the knot (W) travels 2 meters in 1 second, we say it has a _____ of 2 m/s.

6. If the wavelengths were shortened, would the frequency be higher or lower?_____

7. The greatest distance the knot (W) travels from its resting position is called the wave's _____ .

8. What kind of waves are these in the rope?_____

9. A wave in which vibrations from the first disturbance set off a series of collisions followed by calm empty spaces is called a _____ wave.

10. Radiation is the transfer of energy by _____ waves.

11. If the kids were wobbling this rope up and down through pudding instead of air, the _____ would change.

12. The rapid, back and forth movements of any object are called _____ .

13. The frequency of a wave is measured with the unit _____ , which is _____ wave per _____ .

14. If the waves in the rope have a frequency of 2 hertz, how many waves pass a point per second?____

Name

GREAT VIBRATIONS

Waves are rhythmic disturbances or vibrations that carry energy from one place to another. The diagram below shows many different waves that are all similar, except for one thing— their lengths. Their similarity starts all of them belonging to a group of electromagnetic waves. Fill in the blanks to reinforce what you've learned about waves.

1. All the waves shown are _____ waves. (transverse, compressional)

2. The energy produced by electromagnetic waves is _____ .

3. Since the different kinds of waves have different lengths, they also have different _____ .

4. All these waves make up the electromagnetic _____ .

5. The only _____ waves are in the spectrum and in the middle (0.4–0.7 micrometers in length).

6. The kind of light produced by the sun or a "black light" comes from _____ rays.

7. What does it mean to say that a radio station has a frequency of 102 megahertz?_____

8. Which waves have shorter wavelengths: radio waves or X-rays?_____

9. Do gamma rays have a lower or higher frequency than microwaves?_____

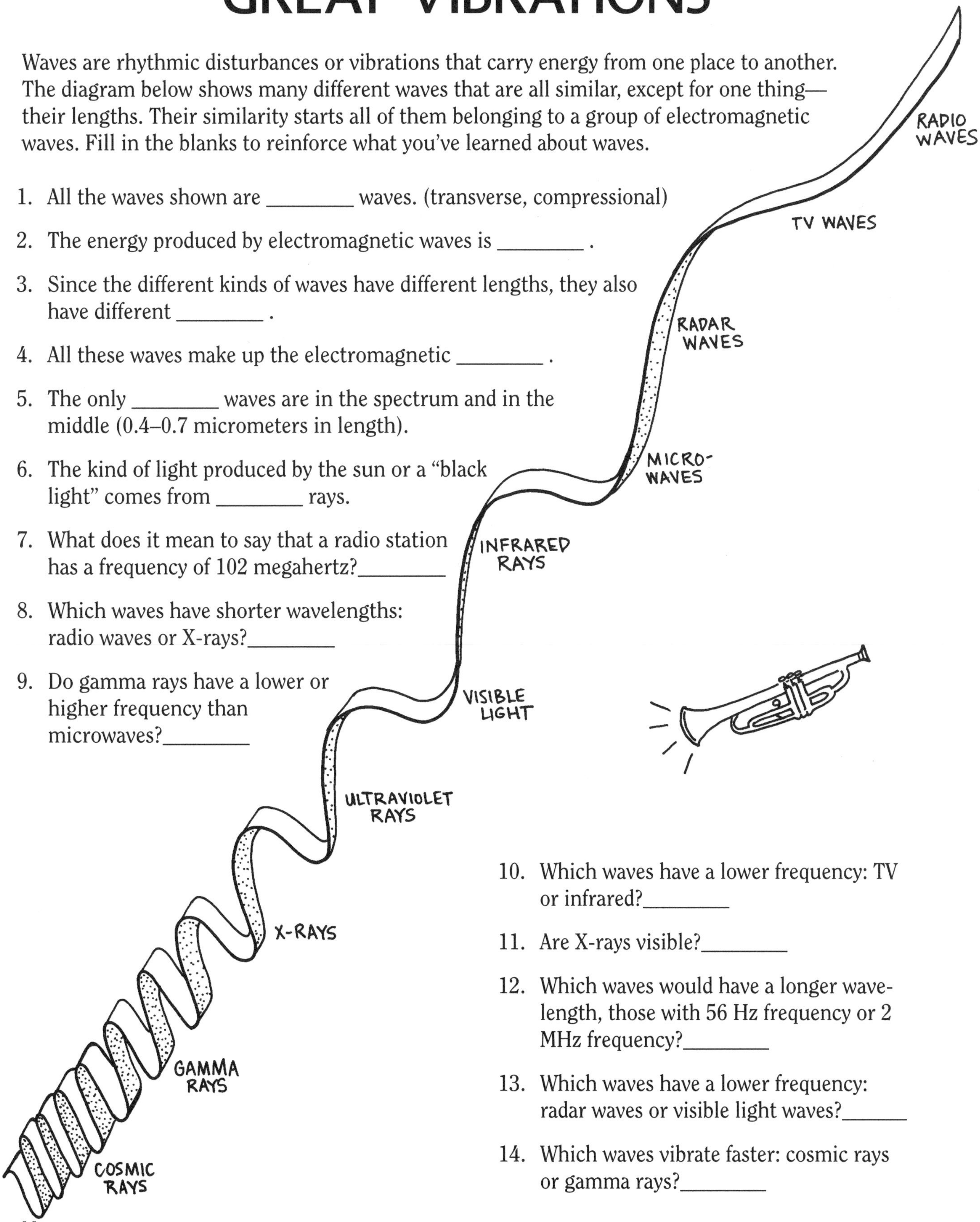

RADIO WAVES

TV WAVES

RADAR WAVES

MICRO-WAVES

INFRARED RAYS

VISIBLE LIGHT

ULTRAVIOLET RAYS

X-RAYS

GAMMA RAYS

COSMIC RAYS

10. Which waves have a lower frequency: TV or infrared?_____

11. Are X-rays visible?_____

12. Which waves would have a longer wavelength, those with 56 Hz frequency or 2 MHz frequency?_____

13. Which waves have a lower frequency: radar waves or visible light waves?_____

14. Which waves vibrate faster: cosmic rays or gamma rays?_____

Name

37

SOUNDS GOOD TO ME

You probably know that your dog can hear sounds you can't hear. So can elephants! Dogs can hear sounds with frequencies higher than those the human ear can pick up. Elephants and other large animals can hear sounds with very low frequencies. People can hear only sound waves that have frequencies of about 20–20,000 hertz.

The scale below shows the loudness of some sounds, measured in decibels (dB). On this scale, each 10-point span is twice as loud as the 10-point category below it. In other words, a sound of 40 dB is twice as loud as sound of 30 dB. A sound of 50 dB is 16 times as loud as a sound of 10 dB.

Sounds begin with a vibration of matter. These vibrations travel outward in compressional waves. Briefly describe each of these features of sound.

1. decibel _____

2. intensity _____

3. loud sound _____

4. soft sound _____

5. amplitude _____

6. loudness _____

7. music _____

8. pitch _____

9. high pitch _____

10. low pitch _____

11. tone quality _____

12. acoustics _____

13. velocity of sound _____

14. frequency of sound _____

15. the Doppler effect _____

ELEPHANTS CAN HEAR VERY LOW FREQUENCIES.

ROCKET LIFT OFF — 170
160
150
140
130
JET TAKE OFF — 120
ROCK MUSIC — 110
THUNDER — 100
POWER MOWER — 90
LOUD ORCHESTRA — 80
MOTOR-CYCLE — 70
60
SHOUT — 50
40
TALKING — 30
CAT'S PURR — 20
WHISPER — 10
PAPER RUSTLE — 0

16. noise _____

_____

DOGS HEAR VERY HIGH FREQUENCIES.

17. reverberation _____

_____

Name _____

IT WORKS FOR BATS

You may have heard that bats find things, not with their eyes, but with the use of sounds. They make use of something called the Doppler effect to find their prey. You use it, too, although you may not know it!

The Doppler effect is a change in wave frequency that is caused when the sound source moves or the person hearing the sound moves. The most frequently occurring instances of this effect in our lives probably are passing sirens and overhead airplanes, but the Doppler effect happens many times a day. Something produces a sound that stays at the same pitch, but to you, because of your motion or the motion of the object, the pitch seems to change (up or down). If you don't already know about the Doppler effect, study it so that you can answer these questions.

1. At which point does the pitch seem higher?

   _____

2. At which point are the sound waves more crowded together? _____

3. At which point does the sound have a lower pitch? _____

6. Whose movement is contributing to the Doppler effect? _____

7. Are the sound waves closer together at point E or F? _____

8. At which point is the pitch higher? _____

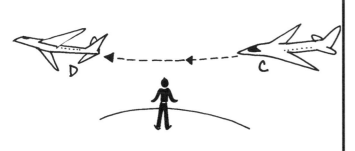

4. Are the sound waves farther apart at point C or D? _____

5. Does the sound have a higher pitch at point C or D? _____

9. Describe the sound waves at point H. _____

   _____

10. At what point is the frequency of the waves lower? _____

11. What happens to the sound as the mower approaches point H? _____

12. What will happen to the sound as the mower turns around and heads back toward the sunbather? _____

   _____

Name _____

ELECTRIFYING FACTS

What is electricity? When electrons move from one atom to another, electricity is produced. Electrons carry negative electric charges. The nucleus of each atom carries positive charges. These charges are attracted to each other, so the electrons want to move where they can join positive charges. Match up these electrifying terms with their descriptions.

_____ A. a circuit with two or more branches for current to flow

_____ B. material that electrons can move through

_____ C. flow of electrons through a conductor

_____ D. made up of series and parallel circuits

_____ E. device to break a circuit

2. static electricity 1. electric charge

3. insulator 4. conductor

7. resistance 6. electric current 5. electroscope

_____ F. poor conductor of electricity

_____ G. unit for measuring rate of electron flow in a circuit

8. battery 9. circuit

_____ H. having too many or too few electrons

_____ I. a temporary source of electric current

11. parallel circuit 10. series circuit

_____ J. rate at which a device converts electrical energy to another form of energy

_____ K. path of electric conductors

_____ L. electric charge built up in one place

12. complex circuit 13. volt

_____ M. device that detects electric charges

_____ N. opposition to the flow of electricity

_____ O. electric circuit where current flows through all parts of the circuit

16. power 15. switch 14. ampere

_____ P. unit to measure electric potential

Name _____

NOT JUST IN LIGHTBULBS

Electricity is in lots of places—including some that may surprise you. These are just a few of the things that can produce electricity. Explain how electricity is produced by or related to each one.

1. CLOTHES JUST OUT OF THE DRYER

2. LIGHTNING

3. AN ELECTRIC EEL

4. WIND

5. A BALLOON AND A SWEATER

6. A PLASTIC COMB AND YOUR DRY HAIR

7. A GLOW WORM

8. SHUFFLING FEET ACROSS A CARPET

9. YOUR BODY

10. RUNNING WATER

Name

KEEPING CURRENT

Are you current on your facts about electric currents and circuits? Show how "current" you are by answering these questions about currents and circuits.

I. A. What is an electric current? _____

_____

  B. What is AC?_____

_____

  C. What is DC? _____

_____

II. _____ 1. Which pictures represent series circuits?

  _____ 2. Which pictures represent parallel circuits?

  _____ 3. In which picture will the bulbs not light up?

  _____ 4. Will the bulbs in C or E be brighter?

  _____ 5. Will the bulbs be dimmer in B or E?

  _____ 6. In F, if the circuit is broken at point X, how many bulbs will light?

  _____ 7. In F, if the circuit is broken at point Z, how many bulbs will light?

  _____ 8. Why do you get a shock if you stick your finger in an electric socket?

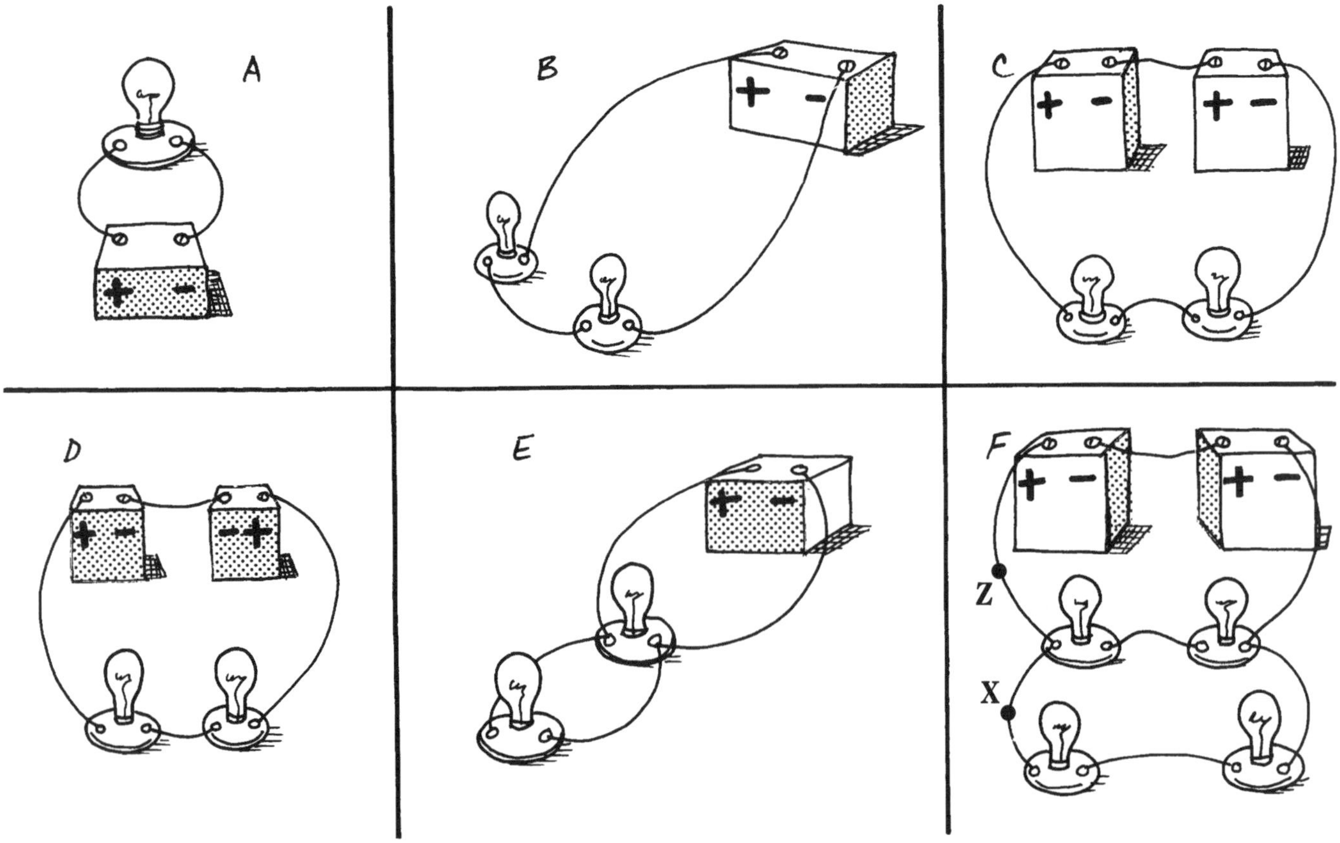

Name _____

WATTS UP?

Electricity wouldn't be nearly as useful if it stayed in the form of electricity. But ingenious devices have been invented which convert electric energy into other forms that can cook your meals, fly you through the air, dry your hair, run your racing boat—even brush your teeth! This is done with the help of **power,** which has to do with the conversion of electric energy into other forms of energy.

Electric power = the rate at which a device can convert electric energy into another form of energy.

Power is calculated by multiplying the current flow (measured in amperes and represented in the formula by **I**) by the voltage (the potential energy, represented by **V**).

$$P = V \times I$$

Electric power is measured in watts.

Use your great science and math skills—along with the formula—to solve these "power" problems.

_____ 1. A source of 120 V sends a current of 13 A (amperes) to a microwave oven to cook some popcorn. How much power is delivered?

_____ 2. Samantha's hair dryer uses 1500 watts of power from a source of 120 V. What is the current?

_____ 3. A source of 120 V sends a 1.25 A current to a lightbulb. How much power is sent?

_____ 4. If your stereo uses 192 watts of power, and a current of 1.6 A flows through it, what is the voltage of the source?

_____ 5. A turkey dinner is cooking in an oven using 2640 watts of power. If a current of 12 A flows through the oven, what is the voltage of the source?

_____ 6. A source of 120 V delivers a current of 0.63 A to a lightbulb. How much power is delivered?

_____ 7. If your television uses 420 watts of power from a 120 V source, what current is flowing through it?

_____ 8. If Brad shaves with 7.2 watts of power from a 120 V source, what current is flowing past his chin?

WHAT WATTAGE !

Approximate Power of Some Home Devices

Lamp	100 watts	Oven	2600 watts
Toaster	100 watts	Stereo	200 watts
Hair Dryer	1600 watts	Microwave	1500 watts
Color TV	200 watts	Lightbulbs	40 watts, 60 watts,
Refrigerator	1000 watts		75 watts, 100 watts, 150 watts
Clock Radio	100 watts		

Name _____

PUZZLING PROPERTIES

Show that you're not puzzled by the various properties of light. This puzzle is made up of words that name characteristics, features, devices, or other things related to the study of light. You'll notice that the puzzle is already finished. But something is missing—the clues. For each word in the puzzle, write a clue that is clear and accurate.

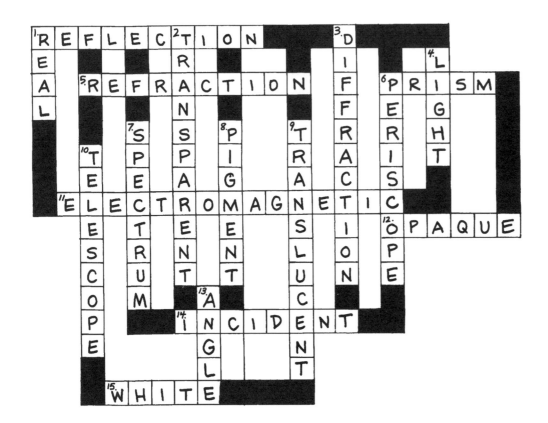

REFRACTION

CLUES

Down

1. _____
2. _____
3. _____
4. _____
6. _____
7. _____
8. _____
9. _____
10. _____
13. _____

Across

1. _____
5. _____
6. _____
11. _____
12. _____
14. _____
15. _____

Name _____

WHY WHITE IS WHITE & BLACK IS BLACK

Is an apple red in the dark? Is the coin on the bottom of the pool right where it appears to be? Can everyone see a whole rainbow? Color is a fascinating feature of light. A rainbow may be the most spectacular display of light's colors, but everyday objects and events remind us of the miracles of light and color. Here's a chance for you to show what you understand about some of the behaviors of light and color.

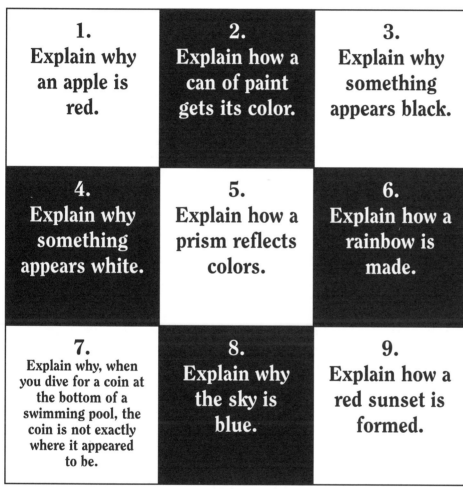

1. Explain why an apple is red.	2. Explain how a can of paint gets its color.	3. Explain why something appears black.
4. Explain why something appears white.	5. Explain how a prism reflects colors.	6. Explain how a rainbow is made.
7. Explain why, when you dive for a coin at the bottom of a swimming pool, the coin is not exactly where it appeared to be.	8. Explain why the sky is blue.	9. Explain how a red sunset is formed.

CAN YOU EXPLAIN THIS TO ME?

*10. Explain why some people insist a rainbow has an indigo band and others say it doesn't.

_____

_____

_____

_____

_____

Extra challenging!

Name _____

LIGHT TRICKS

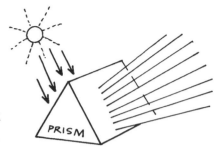

Light plays some spectacular tricks as it travels through Earth's atmosphere. It can make lakes appear out of nowhere in the desert and ships appear to be floating upside-down above the water. Rainbows, mirages, halos, coronas, blue skies, and red skies are all results of the tricks light plays. Match the descriptions of the tricks with the "happenings" below.

_____ 1. mirage

_____ 2. superior mirage

_____ 3. inferior mirage

_____ 4. borealis

_____ 5. blue sky

_____ 6. sunrise and sunset

_____ 7. rainbow

_____ 8. halo

_____ 9. corona

_____ 10. looming, towering, sinking, stooping

_____ 11. green flash

A. This is the most common mirage. A road appears to be wet, or a lake appears in the desert. It happens when air next to Earth is much warmer than the air just above it. Light rays from the sky are refracted and the observer sees the image of the sky turned upside-down (looking like water).

B. A luminous ring around the sun or moon, this phenomenon is caused by refraction of sunlight or moonlight by ice crystals in high clouds. When it's well-developed, three colors show: red (outer), yellow (middle), and green (inner).

C. This optical effect is caused by refraction of light as it passes through layers of the atmosphere that are not alike.

D. As sun rays pass through the thicker layer of the atmosphere closest to Earth's surface, refraction causes short wavelengths (blues and greens) to be scattered out. Only the longest wavelengths at the red end of the spectrum are visible to the observer.

E. This is a small ring around the moon or sun. Diffraction of light by tiny drops of water in clouds spreads light waves around the sun or moon. The outer edge is brown-red; the inner ring is blue-white. Sometimes one is caused by diffraction of dust after a volcanic eruption; the most famous of these is the "Bishop's Ring."

F. Sunlight entering the atmosphere is reflected by millions of dust particles and water drops (a process called scattering). Short wavelengths on the blue end of the spectrum are scattered most, throwing a lot of blue into the atmosphere.

G. Light shines through millions of raindrops which act like tiny prisms by separating white light by refraction into the colors of the spectrum.

H. These optical phenomena are caused by temperature inversions which refract light in a way that changes appearances of objects. Objects appear to be in a different place (higher above or lower below the horizon) or are stretched or decreased in size.

I. These luminous displays of colors and streaks in the sky occur over the poles. They are thought to be caused as streams of sunlight particles bump into ions in the atmosphere and cause them to glow different colors.

J. An image of a ship at sea appears to be floating above the real ship upside-down, with another upright image above it. This phenomenon occurs during a temperature inversion which causes light rays bounding off the ship to be refracted. It happens over cold land or water.

K. This optical phenomenon happens at sunrise or sunset and is seen best over a body of water. Colors at the blue-green end of the spectrum are refracted most and take longer to disappear below the horizon than the red, yellow, and oranges.

Name _____

46

THROUGH LENSES & MIRRORS

When you examine your face in a mirror, take a picture with a camera, look at a bug through a magnifying glass, or spy on your neighbor through a periscope you've made, you're making use of light. In fact, you're counting on light to do some fancy tricks—like reflecting and refracting (bending). Fill in the blanks to complete these simple explanations of the way lenses and mirrors work.

PLANE MIRROR

Light strikes the mirror and is reflected back at an _____(1)_____ from the silver layer at the back.

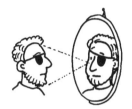

CONVEX MAGNIFYING GLASS

A convex lens is _____(2)_____ in the middle than at the edges. It bends light rays _____(3)_____ to a _____(4)_____ point on the other side of the lens. It can form a real image because it can _____(5)_____ light. A convex lens makes the object appear _____(6)_____ .

CONCAVE LENS

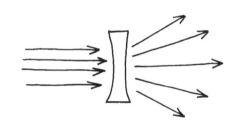

A concave lens is _____(7)_____ in the middle than at the edges. It bends light rays _____(8)_____ from each other. It cannot form a real image because it does not _____(9)_____ light.

PERISCOPE

A periscope is a tube with a _____(10)_____ (or a prism) at each end, set at a _____(11)_____ angle from each other. _____(12)_____ is reflected from the top _____(13)_____ to the bottom _____(14)_____ , so that you can see objects which are _____(15)_____ .

CAMERA

A camera's opening, called an _____(16)_____ , lets light into the camera. A _____(17)_____ focuses the light into an _____(18)_____ onto light-sensitive _____(19)_____ . The image projected is in an _____(20)_____ position.

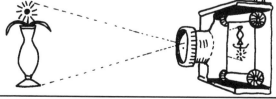

Name

47

THE TRUTH ABOUT MAGNETS

This magnet finds "attractive" only the true statements about magnets and magnetism. Which statements will be attracted to the magnet? Label true statements with a **T**, and label false statements with an **F**. Correct the statements that are false.

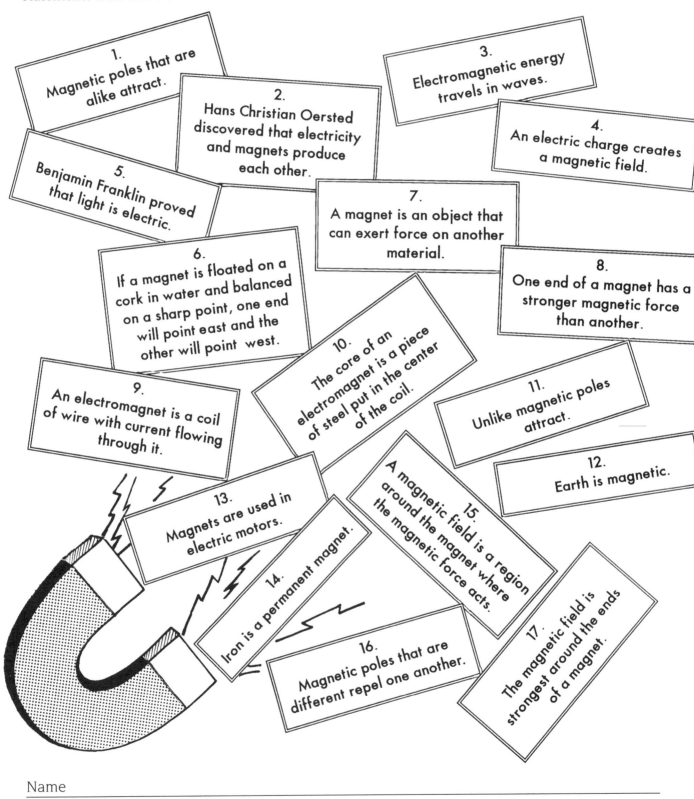

1. Magnetic poles that are alike attract.

2. Hans Christian Oersted discovered that electricity and magnets produce each other.

3. Electromagnetic energy travels in waves.

4. An electric charge creates a magnetic field.

5. Benjamin Franklin proved that light is electric.

6. If a magnet is floated on a cork in water and balanced on a sharp point, one end will point east and the other will point west.

7. A magnet is an object that can exert force on another material.

8. One end of a magnet has a stronger magnetic force than another.

9. An electromagnet is a coil of wire with current flowing through it.

10. The core of an electromagnet is a piece of steel put in the center of the coil.

11. Unlike magnetic poles attract.

12. Earth is magnetic.

13. Magnets are used in electric motors.

14. Iron is a permanent magnet.

15. A magnetic field is a region around the magnet where the magnetic force acts.

16. Magnetic poles that are different repel one another.

17. The magnetic field is strongest around the ends of a magnet.

Name _____

Basic Skills/Physical Science 6-8+

SPEAKING OF PHYSICS

Hidden in this puzzle are 42 words that have to do with physical science. See if you can find them all. All words are written from left to right or top to bottom; none are written backwards. Some words may share a letter. After you find them, choose ten and write a clear definition for them. Use a separate piece of paper or the back of this paper.

```
X  A  R  C  P  M  T  T  O  G  H  E  R  R  S  C
M  P  O  R  T  H  H  A  C  I  D  A  B  K  W  L
A  A  C  C  E  L  E  R  A  T  I  O  N  A  I  W
S  R  C  U  O  L  R  O  T  F  O  R  M  U  L  A
S  A  M  A  T  O  M  O  A  L  E  V  E  R  P  V
S  L  W  O  R  K  A  L  L  P  I  T  C  H  N  E
F  L  E  S  S  N  L  J  Y  P  R  O  T  O  N  L
R  E  E  R  W  A  T  T  S  T  A  T  I  C  B  E
E  L  K  A  S  R  A  T  T  R  O  U  G  H  K  N
Q  R  A  D  M  O  L  E  C  U  L  E  A  J  B  G
U  E  D  I  W  E  D  G  E  C  I  R  C  U  I  T
E  T  R  A  N  S  P  A  R  E  N  T  U  V  C  H
N  S  F  T  E  L  E  M  E  N  T  N  R  E  O  H
C  H  S  I  M  O  T  I  O  N  O  B  R  L  M  E
Y  F  S  O  L  U  T  I  O  N  S  G  E  O  P  R
P  C  O  N  D  E  N  S  A  T  I  O  N  C  O  T
M  I  X  T  U  R  E  Y  O  V  O  L  T  I  U  Z
I  N  S  U  L  A  T  I  O  N  F  H  G  T  N  P
E  L  E  C  T  R  O  N  A  F  G  H  O  Y  D  T
D  O  P  P  L  E  R  A  A  G  R  A  V  I  T  Y
F  U  L  C  R  U  M  A  C  H  I  N  E  P  O  D
N  U  C  L  E  U  S  T  H  K  I  N  E  T  I  C
O  P  A  Q  U  E  L  E  C  T  R  I  C  I  T  Y
```

Name

Basic Skills/Physical Science 6-8+

PRACTICALLY PHYSICS

Officially, *technology* is the application of science for practical purposes. The world of physical science has been put to practical use in thousands or millions of ways with contraptions, machines, and creative innovations. Here are just a few of the thousands of inventions, systems, or processes that make use of physical science. Choose two to investigate. Find out how physical science is connected to or used by them. Write a summary of what you've found. (You may add your own ideas to this list!)

Name

APPENDIX

CONTENTS

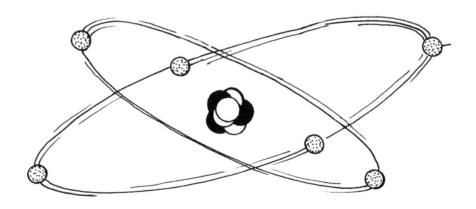

PERIODIC TABLE

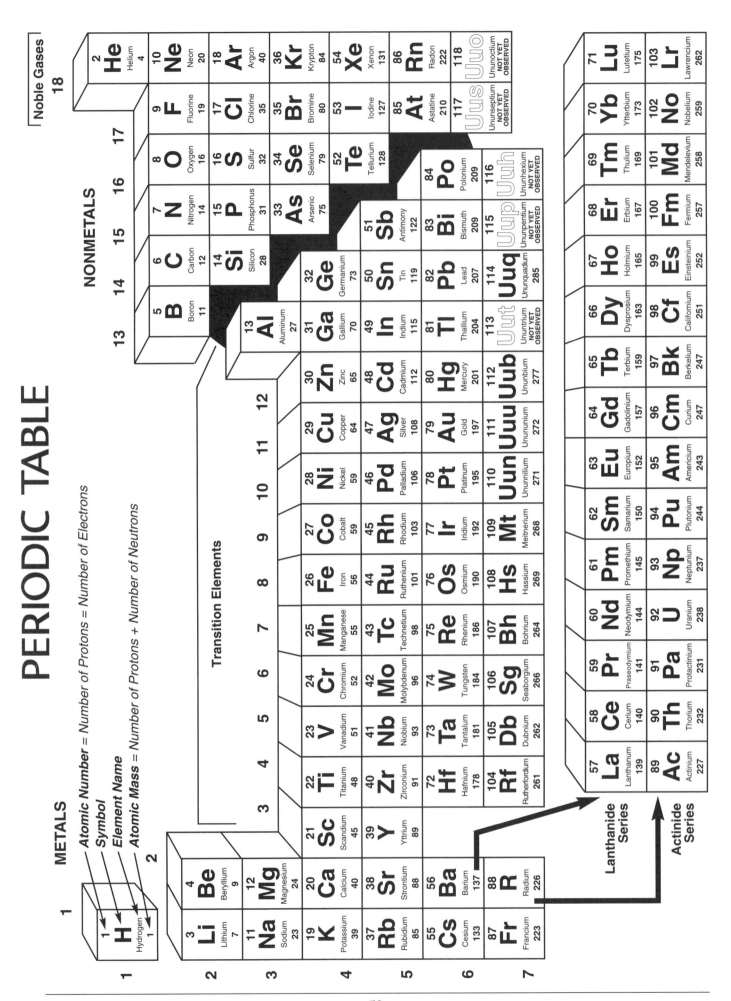

METALS

Atomic Number = Number of Protons = Number of Electrons
Symbol
Element Name
Atomic Mass = Number of Protons + Number of Neutrons

NONMETALS

Noble Gases

Transition Elements

Lanthanide Series

Actinide Series

Basic Skills/Physical Science 6-8+

Copyright ©1997 by Incentive Publications, Inc., Nashville, TN.

GLOSSARY OF PHYSICAL SCIENCE TERMS

absolute zero: zero on the Kelvin temperature scale; the coldest possible temperature

acceleration: the rate at which velocity changes

acid: a substance that produces hydronium ions when dissolved in water

acoustics: the study of sound and its effect on people

action-reaction pairs: two forces having equal strength in opposite directions

air resistance: the force of air against a moving object

alloy: a material that contains more than one element and has metallic properties

alternating current (AC): a continuous back and forth movement of electrons in a circuit

ampere (A): the rate of electron flow in a circuit

amplify: to increase the amplitude of a wave; or to increase the volume of sound or the strength of an electric current

amplitude: the greatest distance the particles in a wave rise or fall from their rest position

angle of incidence: the angle made between a wave striking a surface and the normal angle to the surface

angle of reflection: the angle between a reflected wave and the normal angle to the surface from which it is reflected

anode (+): the positive electrode in an electrical circuit

aqueous solution: solution with water as the solvent

Archimedes' principle: the buoyant force on an object submerged in a fluid is equal to the weight of the fluid displaced by that object

atom: the smallest unit of an element that has all the properties of that element

atomic mass: mass of an atom

atomic number: the number of protons in the nucleus of an atom

average speed: the total distance an object travels divided by the total time it takes to travel the distance

balanced forces: forces acting on the same body equal in strength but acting in opposite directions

base: a substance that increases the hydroxide ion concentration when added to water

battery: two or more wet or dry cells that produce an electric current

binary compound: a compound composed of only two elements

biochemistry: the study of the chemistry of living systems

boiling point: the temperature at which a substance changes rapidly from a liquid to a gas

bond: an attraction between atoms or ions that is the result of gaining, losing, or sharing electrons by atoms

buoyant force: the upward force of a fluid on an object in it

catalyst: a substance that increases the rate of a chemical reaction without being permanently changed itself

Celsius (C): the temperature scale on which 0° is the freezing point of water and 100° is the boiling point

centripetal force: a force on an object acting toward the center of a circular path

chemical change: change in which a substance becomes another substance having different properties

chemical formula: a group of chemical symbols that tells the atoms in a compound and their ratios

chemical properties: characteristics of a substance that determine how it reacts to form other substances

circuit: a closed-loop path of conduction through which an electric current flows

circuit breaker: device that stops the flow of current before wires in a circuit get too hot

colloid: a mixture with particle size between that of solutions and suspensions

compass: a suspended magnet with one end pointing toward Earth's magnetic north pole

compound: a substance containing atoms of two or more elements chemically combined

concave lens: a lens that is thinner in the middle than at the edges and refracts light rays away from each other

concentration: the amount of solute per unit volume of solvent

condensation: the change from a gas to a liquid

conduction: energy transferred through matter from particle to particle, mostly in solids

conductor: material electrons can move through

convection: the transfer of thermal energy by the actual movement of the warmed matter; occurs in liquids and gases

convex lens: a lens thicker in the middle than at the edges; refracts light rays toward each other

core: a piece of iron in the center of a coil making a stronger electromagnet

corrosion: a destructive chemical change in a metal such as rusting

crystal: a solid material having a regular repeating geometric form

current: the flow of electrons in a conductor

decibel (dB): the unit of measure for the volume or loudness of sound

density: the mass of a material divided by its volume

diffraction: the bending of waves as they pass through an opening or around the edge of an object

direct current (DC): flow of electrons in one direction through a conductor

distillation: physical separation of the parts of a liquid through vaporization and condensation

Doppler effect: a change in wave frequency caused by the motion of the wave sound source or the movement of the observer

effort force: the force you apply to the machine

electric current: the flow of electrons or other charged particles through a conductor

electrolysis: any chemical change produced by an electric current

electromagnet: a soft iron core surrounded by a wire coil through which an electric current passes, magnetizing the core

electron: a negatively charged particle that orbits around the nucleus of an atom

electron cloud: region around the nucleus occupied by electrons

element: a substance made up of one kind of atom; cannot be broken down by physical or chemical means

evaporation: change from a liquid to a gas at the liquid surface

filter: a device used to separate parts of a mixture; a transparent material that separates colors of light

force: a push or pull one body exerts on another

formula: combination of chemical atomic symbols showing the atoms present in a compound and their ratio

freezing: changing from liquid to solid

freezing point: temperature at which a liquid changes to a solid

frequency: the number of waves that pass a point in a given unit of time

friction: a force that opposes motion between two surfaces that are touching each other

fulcrum: the point on which a lever rotates or pivots

generator: a machine that changes mechanical energy into electrical energy

geothermal energy: heat from within the earth

gravity: the mutual force of attraction that exists on all objects in the universe; the force Earth exerts on all objects near it

group (family): a vertical column in the Periodic Table; elements within a group have similar chemical properties

heat: energy transferred between objects because of a difference in temperature, from high temperature to low temperature

hydrocarbon: a compound containing only carbon and hydrogen

hydroelectric power: electric power generated by moving water

image: the reproduction of an object formed with lenses or with mirrors

inclined plane: a simple machine which is a slanted surface used to raise objects

indicator: organic compound that changes color in an acid or a base

inertia: the property of a body that resists any change in velocity

insulation: a material used to slow the flow of heat or electricity

intensity: a measurement of amplitude of sound; expressed using decibels

isomers: compounds having the same molecular formula but different structural formulas

isotopes: atoms of the same element with different numbers of neutrons

joule (J): a unit for measuring work or energy

kelvin: SI unit of temperature

kilowatt: equals 1000 watts; a watt is a very small unit of power

kilowatt-hour (kWh): a unit used to measure electrical energy equal to 1000 watt-hours

kinetic energy: energy of motion

kinetic theory of matter: all matter is made up of tiny particles that are in constant motion; spacing of the particles determines the state of the matter

law of conservation of energy: energy can change from one form to another, but can never be created or destroyed

law of conservation of mass: mass is neither gained nor lost in a chemical change

lens: a curved, transparent object, usually made of glass or clear plastic

lever: a simple machine consisting of an effort arm, fulcrum, and resistance arm

light: the only visible part of the electro-magnetic spectrum

liquid: the state of matter having a constant volume but no definite shape

litmus paper: an indicator that turns red in acid and blue in base

loudness: the intensity of sound; loud sounds produce sound waves with a large amplitude

machine: a device that makes work easier by changing the speed, direction, or amount of a force

magnet: any object that has a magnetic field and is able to exert forces on other magnets

magnetic field: area of magnetic lines of force

magnetic poles: locations of the strongest magnetic force, usually at opposite ends of the magnet

mass: the amount of matter in an object; the measure of the inertia of a body

mass number: the sum of protons and neutrons in an atom

mechanical advantage (MA): the amount by which the applied force is multiplied by a machine

mechanical energy: the kinetic energy and potential energy of lifting, bending, and stretching

melting: change from a solid to a liquid

melting point: the temperature at which a substance changes from a solid to a liquid

metals: elements whose atoms generally have three or fewer electrons in their outer energy level

microwaves: very short wavelength radio waves

mixture: two or more elements or compounds that are blended without combining chemically

molecule: neutral particle formed by atoms bonded covalently; may be an element or a compound

motion: change in position

motor: device that converts electrical energy into mechanical energy

net force: force that results from unbalanced forces acting on an object and changes in the motion of an object

neutral: neither acid nor base; not electrically charged

neutron: particle in the nucleus of an atom; has no charge

newton (N): the unit of force

noise: sounds produced by irregular or unpleasant or unwanted vibrations

nonmetal: an element with five or more electrons in the outer energy level

nuclear energy: energy produced by the splitting of the nuclei of atoms

nucleus: the central portion of an atom containing neutrons and protons

opaque: material that absorbs light

ore: a mineral or other natural from which one or more metals may be profitably obtained

organic chemistry: the study of carbon and its compounds

organic compounds: compounds that contain carbon, usually bonded to hydrogen

parallel circuit: a circuit in which two or more conductors are connected across two common points in the circuit to provide separate conducting paths for the current

Periodic Table: an arrangement of the chemical elements in rows according to increasing atomic numbers, in vertical columns having similar properties

pH: a number that shows acidity; a measure of hydronium ion concentration in a solution

physical change: a change in size, shape, color, or state; a change without a change in chemical composition

physical property: a characteristic of matter that may be observed without changing the chemical composition of the substance

physical science: the study of matter and energy

pigment: a colored material that absorbs certain colors of light and reflects other colors

pitch: a quality of a sound determined by its frequency

potential energy: the energy due to position or condition

power: amount of work done per unit of time

precipitate: insoluble substance that crystallizes out of solution

pressure: amount of force per unit area

prism: an object of transparent material with two straight faces at an angle to each other which refracts light to produce a visible light spectrum

property: a feature of matter or the way it acts

proton: a positively charged particle in the nucleus of an atom

pulley: a simple machine

radiant energy: energy that can travel through space in the form of waves

radiation: transfer of energy that does not require matter; energy released from atoms and molecules in nuclear reaction; the transfer of energy by electromagnetic waves

radioactivity: the emitting of high energy radiation or particles from nuclei of radioactive atoms

radio waves: radiation having the lowest frequencies and the longest wavelengths

reactant: a substance that undergoes a chemical change

reflection: bouncing of a wave or ray off a surface

refraction: bending of a wave or light ray, caused by a decrease in speed as it passes from one material into another

resistance: any opposition that slows down or prevents movement of electrons through a conductor; opposition to the flow of electricity

resistance force: the force exerted by the machine

salt: compound containing a positive ion from a base and a negative ion from an acid

saturated: solution contains the maximum amount of solute for a given temperature

screw: a simple machine which is an inclined plane wound around a cylinder

semiconductor: a material with a resistance between that of a conductor and an insulator; conducts electric current weakly

series circuit: an electric circuit in which the parts are connected so that the same current flows through all parts of the circuit

simple machine: a device that makes work easier by changing the speed, direction, or amount of force; it consists of only one machine

solar energy: energy or radiation from the sun

solubility: the amount of a substance (solute) that will dissolve in a specific amount of another substance (solvent) at a given temperature

solute: the substance dissolved in a solvent

solution: a homogeneous mixture in which one substance (solute) is dissolved in another substance (solvent)

solvent: the substance in which a solute is dissolved

sound wave: a compressional wave produced by vibrations

speed: rate of change of the position of an object; rate of motion

static electricity: electricity produced by charged bodies; charge built up in one place

supersaturated: solution contains more solute than would normally dissolve at a given temperature

suspension: heterogeneous mixture in which the particles are large enough to be seen; particles will eventually settle out

symbol: the shorthand way to write the name of an element

temperature: a measure of average kinetic energy of the particles of a material; usually measured with a thermometer

thermal energy: the total energy of all the particles in an object

tone quality: differences among sound of the same pitch and loudness

translucent: material that transmits light, but does not allow you to see clearly through it

transparent: having the property of transmitting or passing light

transverse wave: wave in which matter vibrates at right angles to the direction in which the wave travels

trough: the valley of a wave

ultraviolet radiation: invisible radiation that has a shorter wavelength than light; next to violet light in the electromagnetic spectrum

unsaturated: solution can dissolve more solute

vaporization: the change from a liquid to a gas

velocity: the speed and direction of a moving object

vibration: rapid back and forth movement

viscosity: the property of a liquid that describes how it pours

visible light spectrum: band of colors produced by a prism

volt (V): the SI unit of electric potential

volume: loudness of a sound

watt (W): the SI unit of power; one watt is one joule of work per second

wave: rhythmic disturbance that carries energy; transfers energy from one place to another

wavelength: the distance between a point on one wave to the same identical point on the next wave

wedge: a simple machine that is an inclined plane with either one or two sloping sides

weight: the force of gravity that Earth exerts on an object resting on its surface

wheel and axle: a simple machine that is a variation of the lever; consists of a large wheel fixed to a smaller wheel that rotates together

work: the transfer of energy as a result of motion of objects

work input: the effort force multiplied by the effort distance

work output: the resistance force multiplied by the resistance distance

PHYSICAL SCIENCE
SKILLS TEST

Each correct answer is worth 1 point. Total Score Possible = 100 points.

For questions 1–6, use these segments from the Periodic Table to answer the questions.

A.
23
Na
11

B.
64
Cu
29

C.
1
H
1

1. What element is shown in A? _____

2. What is the atomic number of B? _____

3. What is the atomic mass of A? _____

4. How many electrons does hydrogen have? ____

5. What element is shown in B? _____

6. How many neutrons are in element A? _____

For questions 7–16, match the correct term with each definition below. Write the letter of the correct answer.

A. suspension	F. acid
B. pH	G. neutralization
C. condensation	H. base
D. solute	I. viscosity
E. volume	J. electrons

____ 7. amount of mass

____ 8. heterogeneous mixture in which particles can be seen

____ 9. process of combining a base with an acid

____ 10. scale for measuring acidity

____ 11. shared when elements combine to form a compound

____ 12. change from a gas to a liquid

____ 13. compound that produces hydronium ions in water solution

____ 14. ability of liquid to be poured

____ 15. substance dissolved in a solvent

____ 16. the chemical opposite of an acid

For questions 17–19, for each formula show the name of each element and the number of atoms represented by the formula:

Ex: C_2H_2 = 2 carbon atoms + 2 hydrogen atoms

17. $CaSO_4$ _____

18. NH_3 _____

19. NaO_2 _____

For questions 20–22, use the diagram below to answer these questions. Write the letter of the correct answer on the line.

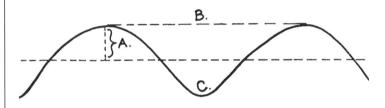

_____ 20. Which letter is in the trough?

_____ 21. Which letter represents the amplitude of a wave?

_____ 22. Which letter represents wavelength?

For questions 23–32, write the letter of the correct answer on the line.

____ 23. The particle in an atom that has no electric charge is the ____ .
    a. electron   c. proton
    b. neutron   d. electron cloud

____ 24. The atomic mass of an element is equal to this:
    a. # of protons
    b. # of neutrons
    c. # of protons + electrons
    d. # of neutrons + protons

____ 25. Groups on the Periodic Table with similar properties are ____ .
    a. families   c. tables
    b. periods   d. compounds

Name _____

Basic Skills/Physical Science 6-8+   Copyright ©1997 by Incentive Publications, Inc., Nashville, TN.

___ 26. Particles found in an atom other than protons, neutrons, and electrons are ____ .
    a. polymers   c. quarks
    b. isotopes   d. acids

___ 27. If an element has 18 electrons, how many would be in the third energy level?
    a. 16   c. 10
    b. 8   d. 2

___ 28. What state of matter has no definite shape and no definite volume?
    a. gas   c. liquid
    b. solid   d. element

___ 29. At what point does a liquid change to a gas?
    a. freezing point   c. dew point
    b. melting point   d. boiling point

___ 30. Molecules will move faster and farther apart when state changes from
    a. liquid to solid   c. gas to solid
    b. gas to liquid   d. liquid to gas

___ 31. When a container decreases in size, what will happen to an amount of gas in the container?
    a. temperature of the gas will decrease
    b. volume of the gas will increase
    c. pressure gas exerts on the container will increase
    d. pressure gas exerts on the container will decrease

___ 32. Two or more elements bonded together chemically form a
    a. mixture   c. compound
    b. colloid   d. suspension

For questions 33–35, write the correct answer for these problems with rate, time, and distance.

_____ 33. Two trains are traveling toward each other from 800 miles apart, each at 80 miles per hour. How long will it be before they meet?

_____ 34. The *Speed Chaser* covers 1350 miles in 15 hours. What is its rate?

_____ 35. The *Silver Streak* travels at a rate of 102 mph for 6 hours. What distance is covered?

For questions 36–47, write the name of the element or compound that is represented by the symbol.

36. Fe _____

37. N _____

38. O_2 _____

39. NaCl _____

40. C _____

41. CO _____

42. Au _____

43. Ca _____

44. He _____

45. HCl _____

46. CO_2 _____

47. Hg _____

For questions 48–50, use the diagrams of circuits to answer these questions.

___ 48. Which circuit(s) is/are parallel?

___ 49. Which circuit(s) is/are series?

___ 50. In which example will a light be unlikely to light up?

For questions 51–60, match the correct term with each definition below. Write the correct letter on the line.

    A. centripetal   F. friction
    B. conduction   G. convection
    C. inertia   H. acceleration
    D. momentum   I. kinetic
    E. velocity   J. mechanical advantage

___ 51. speed and direction of moving object

___ 52. tendency of a body to resist change in velocity

___ 53. mass of an object multiplied by its velocity

___ 54. transfer of energy from particle to particle through matter

___ 55. rate of change in velocity

___ 56. energy of motion

Name _____

___ 57. force that opposes motion of two touching surfaces

___ 58. force pulling toward the center of a circular path

___ 59. transfer of energy through movement of a fluid

___ 60. increase in amount of work done with help of a machine

For questions 61–63, use the diagram below to answer these questions.

___ 61. At which point are the sound waves closer together?

___ 62. At which point is the pitch of the sound lowest?

___ 63. At which point is the pitch of the sound highest?

For questions 64–66, write the correct answer on the line.

___ 64. Jana is drying her hair using a 120 V source of power with a current of 12.5 A. How many watts of power is her hairdryer using?

___ 65. The oven is baking a cake using a current of 12 A and 2640 watts of power. What is the voltage of the power source?

___ 66. If your stereo uses 2 A of current from a power source of 120 V, what is the wattage of power it's using?

For questions 67–69, use the diagram of the electromagnetic wave below to answer these questions.

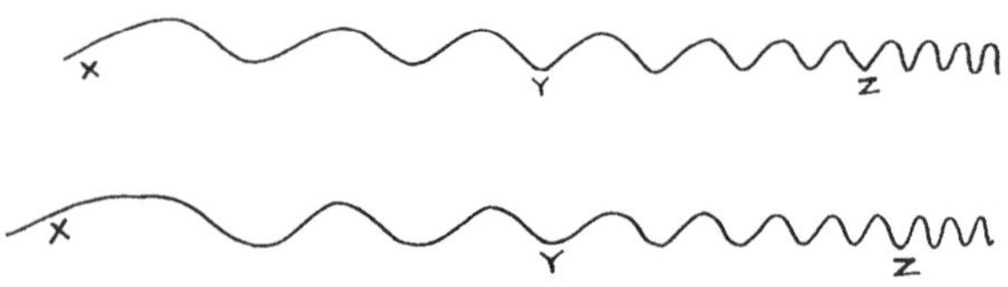

___ 67. Which point would represent visible light waves?

___ 68. Which point would represent gamma rays?

___ 69. Which point would represent radio waves?

For questions 70–78, match the correct term with each definition following.

A. direct current   D. potential   G. filter
B. indicator   E. insulator   H. effort force
C. distillation   F. lipid   I. density

___ 70. energy due to position or condition of matter

___ 71. substance that does not conduct heat or electricity well

___ 72. mass of a material divided by its volume

___ 73. flow of electricity in one direction

___ 74. force applied to a machine

___ 75. separation of liquids by vaporization and condensation

___ 76. device for separating parts of a mixture

___ 77. organic compound which changes color in an acid or base

___ 78. class of organic compounds that contains fats and oils

For questions 79–81, write the chemical formula for each molecule.

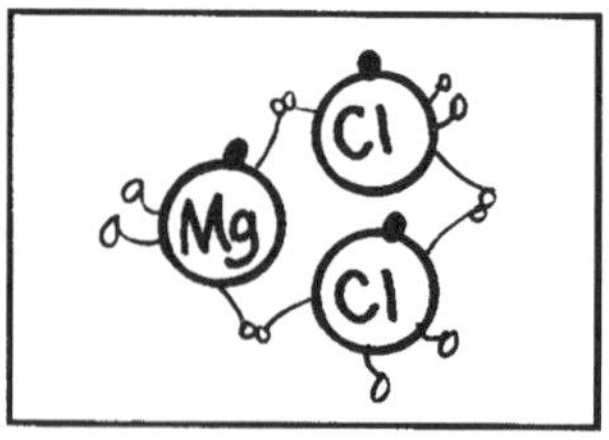

79. _____

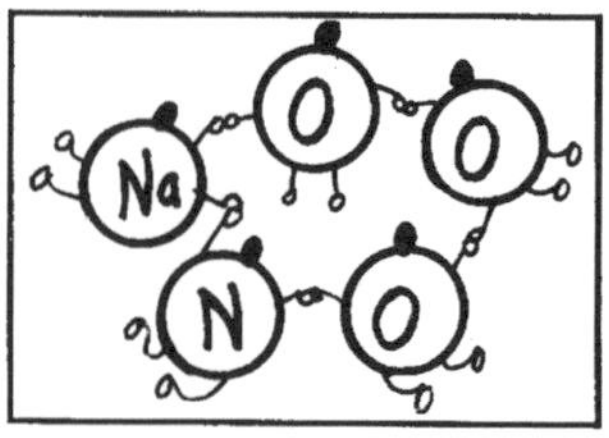

80. _____

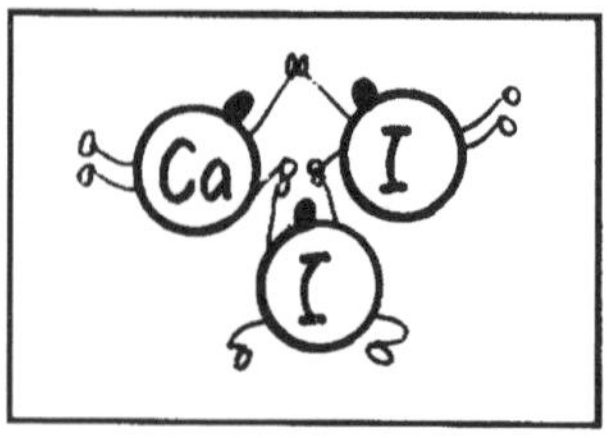

81. _____

Name _____

For questions 82–91, write the letter of the correct answer on the line.

___ 82. Which is not a physical change?
   a. melting butter
   b. whipping cream
   c. mixing lemonade
   d. molding bread

___ 83. Which is not a chemical change?
   a. boiling, evaporating water
   b. burned toast
   c. rusting nails
   d. bleaching your hair

___ 84. Which is not an organic compound?
   a. vitamin
   b. starch
   c. sulfuric acid
   d. protein
   e. carbohydrate

___ 85. A substance that speeds up a chemical reaction without changing itself is a(n)
   a. catalyst
   b. inhibitor
   c. acid
   d. lipid

___ 86. Which will turn red when dipped in an acidic solution?
   a. red litmus
   b. blue litmus
   c. both
   d. neither

___ 87. What causes a spaceship to get red-hot when reentering Earth's atmosphere?
   a. inertia
   b. friction
   c. pressure
   d. momentum

___ 88. What is the greatest distance a wave travels from its resting position?
   a. pitch
   b. wavelength
   c. amplitude
   d. frequency

___ 89. Which gives opposition to the flow of electricity?
   a. a resistance   c. a conductor
   b. a circuit   d. an ampere

___ 90. What term refers to the bending of light as it passes through an opening or around a bend?
   a. reflecting   c. radiation
   b. refraction   d. diffraction

___ 91. Unit for measuring electric power:
   a. hertz   c. newton
   b. kelvin   d. watt

For questions 92–96, write the correct answer on the line.

92. What happens to a wavelength as the frequency of a wave increases?

_____

_____ 93. Which has a higher frequency, a TV wave or an X-ray?

_____ 94. What unit is used to measure wave frequencies?

_____ 95. What kind of energy is transferred by electromagnetic waves?

_____ 96. What term means the rapid movement of particles back and forth?

For questions 97–100, use the drawings below to answer these questions.

___ 97. What point is the fulcrum?

___ 98. What point is the effort force?

___ 99. What point is the resistance force?

100. What simple machine is this? _____

SCORE: Total Points _____ out of a possible 100 points

Name _____

PHYSICAL SCIENCE
SKILLS TEST ANSWER KEY

1. sodium
2. 64
3. 11
4. 1
5. copper
6. 12
7. E
8. A
9. G
10. B
11. J
12. C
13. F
14. I
15. D
16. H
17. 1 calcium atom + 1 sulfur atom + 4 oxygen atoms
18. 1 nitrogen atom + 3 hydrogen atoms
19. 1 sodium atom + 2 oxygen atoms
20. C
21. A
22. B
23. b
24. d
25. a
26. c
27. b
28. a
29. d
30. d
31. c

32. c
33. 5 hours
34. 90 mph
35. 612 miles
36. iron
37. nitrogen
38. oxygen
39. sodium chloride
40. carbon
41. carbon monoxide
42. gold
43. calcium
44. helium
45. hydrogen chloride
46. carbon dioxide
47. mercury
48. B
49. C
50. C
51. E
52. C
53. D
54. B
55. H
56. I
57. F
58. A
59. G
60. J
61. A
62. B
63. A
64. 1500 watts
65. 220 V
66. 240 watts

67. Y
68. Z
69. X
70. D
71. E
72. I
73. A
74. H
75. C
76. G
77. B
78. F
79. $MgCl_2$
80. $NaNO_3$
81. CaI_2
82. d
83. a
84. c
85. a
86. b
87. b
88. c
89. a
90. d
91. d
92. gets shorter
93. X-ray
94. hertz
95. radiation
96. vibration
97. Q
98. R
99. P
100. lever

ANSWERS

Page 10

I. a. nucleus   c. neutron
   b. electron   d. proton

II. 1. neutron   5. 8
   2. proton   6. 18
   3. electron   7. electrons; protons
   4. 2   8. protons (or electrons)

Check to see that student model has 8 protons and 8 neutrons in the nucleus, 2 electrons in the first orbit, and 6 in the second orbit.

Page 11

A. carbon   F. hydrogen
B. neon   G. lithium
C. boron   H. nitrogen
D. oxygen   I. beryllium
E. helium

Page 12

1. a. 1   7. a. Na
   b. 1   b. 12
2. a. magnesium   c. sodium
   b. 12   8. a. 78
3. a. 26   b. 117
   b. Fe   9. a. lead
4. a. 5   b. 82
   b. boron   10. a. 40
5. a. 79   b. 91
   b. 79   11. a. 88
   c. 79   b. 138
   d. gold   12. a. 64
6. a. 59   b. 35
   b. Ni

Page 13

1. chlorine; Cl   11. mercury; Hg
2. manganese; Mn   12. potassium; K
3. krypton; Kr   13. calcium; Ca
4. boron; B   14. radon; Rn
5. sulfur; S   15. lithium; Li
6. iron; Fe   16. cobalt; Co
7. sodium; Na   17. barium; Ba
8. copper; Cu   18. oxygen; O
9. neon; Ne   19. helium; He
10. zirconium; Zr   20. strontium; Sr

Page 14

1. no
2. positive
3. negative
4. region around the nucleus that contains electrons
5. different orbits occupied by electrons
6. 2nd
7. no
8. no
9. 32
10. 6

Page 15 (continued from column 2)

11. 3
12. an atom with a number of neutrons different from the usual atom of that element
13. yes
14. yes
15. smaller particles (than atoms) of matter that make up protons and neutrons
   A. 6; 2; 4; 0   E. 10; 2; 8; 0
   B. 80; 2; 8; 18   F. 33; 2; 8; 18
   C. 20; 2; 8; 10   G. 11; 2; 8; 1
   D. 36; 2; 8; 18

Page 15

1. families   12. iron
2. properties   13. mercury
3. halogen   14. ore
4. noble gas   15. alloy
5. periods   16. aluminum
6. different   17. hydrogen
7. metals   18. allotrope
8. nonmetals   19. silicon
9. transition   20. helium
10. two   21. organic
11. alkali   22. carbon

Page 16

Across	Down
1. Th: Thorium	1. Ti: Titanium
2. As: Arsenic	2. Ar: Argon
3. Zr: Zirconium	3. Zn: Zinc
4. Li: Lithium	4. La: Lanthanum
5. Br: Bromide	5. Ba: Barium
6. Sn: Tin	6. Si: Silicon
7. Ca: Calcium	7. Cu: Copper
8. Ni: Nickel	8. Na: Sodium
9. C: Carbon	10. Al: Aluminium
10. Au: Gold	11. Rn: Radon
11. Ra: Radium	12. Kr: Krypton
12. K: Potassium	14. Mg: Magnesium
13. Cl: Chlorine	15. Fe: Iron
14. Mn: Manganese	16. He: Helium
15. Fr: Francium	18. Nb: Niobium
16. Hg: Mercury	19. Po: Polonium
17. N: Nitrogen	
18. Ne: Neon	
19. Pt: Platinum	
20. H: Hydrogen	
21. Pb: Lead	
22. Co: Cobalt	
23. O: Oxygen	
24. F: Fluoride	

Page 17

Student should describe each of the 3 ordinary states of matter:

I. A. Solids—have shape and volume; molecules are packed tightly together and vibrate back and forth only slightly.

B. Liquids—have volume but no shape; take the shape of their container; molecules are farther apart than in a solid, but still attract each other.

C. Gases—have no specific volume and no shape; molecules fill whatever space available; molecules and their particles move around very fast and don't necessarily stay very attracted to each other.

II. 1. B   3. A   5. E
   2. D   4. C

III. Plasma can exist only at extremely high temperatures; its particles move very fast

Page 18

Explanations will vary for these changes in matter. See that student explanations include a description of the state changes below, a description of the movement of the particles, a statement of the effects of temperature change.

1. liquid to solid   6. gas to liquid
2. liquid to gas   7. liquid to gas
3. solid to liquid   8. solid to liquid
4. solid to liquid   9. liquid to solid
5. liquid to gas

Page 19

Untrue statements (corrected) are:

2. Mass = amount of a substance; Weight = measure of the pull of gravity on a substance
3. Density = mass divided by volume
7. larger particles
8. can be seen with the eye or microscope
10. All matter takes up space.
11. physical property
13. chemical property
17. property of a liquid

Pages 20-21

1. HCl   8. $CaCO_3$ 15. PbO
2. H_2O 9. $NaHCO_3$ 16. H_2SO_4
3. CO_2 10. $AgNO_3$ 17. HBr
4. P_2O_5 11. CH_4 18. HF
5. NH_3 12. Na_2O_2 19. AgCl
6. H_2O_2 13. CO   20. NaCl
7. SiO_2 14. NO_2

Page 22

1. P   9. C   17. C
2. P   10. P   18. C
3. C   11. P   19. C
4. P   12. P   20. P
5. P   13. P   21. C
6. P   14. P   22. P
7. P   15. C
8. C   16. P

Page 23

1. hydrogen
2. alkali or base
3. polymer
4. acid
5. acids
6. lipids
7. alkali or base
8. enzyme
9. proteins
10. carbon dioxide
11. alkalis or bases
12. carbohydrate
13. pH
14. isomers
15. acid
16. alkali or base
17. hydrocarbon
18. phenolphthalein
19. sugar, starch
20. acid
21. amino acids, lipids, vitamins
22. unsaturated
23. saturated
24. neutralization
25. vitamins

Page 24

MATTER
1. What are solids, liquids, and gases?
2. What are gases?
3. What are liquids?
4. What are solids?
5. What are crystals?
6. What is viscosity?

ELEMENTS
7. What is an atom?
8. What is an atomic number?
9. What is an electron cloud?
10. What are metals?
11. What is hydrogen?
12. What are transition elements?

COMPOUNDS
13. What is a chemical change?
14. What is a chemical formula?
15. What is a molecule?
16. What is an ion?
17. What is hydrogen peroxide?
18. What is $MgCl_2$?

PHYSICAL CHANGES
19. What is a melting point?
20. What is a boiling point?
21. What is a freezing point?
22. What is condensation?
23. What is evaporation?
24. What is temperature?

Page 25

MIXTURES & SOLUTIONS
1. What is a solvent?
2. What is solubility?
3. What is a saturated solution?
4. What is heterogeneous?
5. What is a suspension?
6. What is distillation?

CHEMICAL REACTIONS
7. What is a catalyst?
8. What is energy?
9. What is an inhibitor?
10. What is a chemical equation?
11. What is a precipitate?
12. What is a synthesis reaction?

ORGANIC CHEMISTRY
13. What is carbon?
14. What are hydrocarbons?
15. What are isomers?
16. What is a polymer?
17. What is a carbohydrate?
18. What is an amino acid?

ACIDS, BASES, & SALTS
19. What is an acid?
20. What is litmus paper?
21. What is pH?
22. What is ammonia?
23. What is sodium hydroxide?
24. What is a salt?

Page 27

1. acceleration
2. velocity
3. mass
4. terminal
5. horizontal
6. centripetal
7. speed
8. rate
9. inertia
10. rest
11. momentum
12. air resistance
13. vertical
14. newtons
15. force
16. pairs
17. direction
18. gravity
19. friction
20. pressure

Page 28

1st: rest; rest; moving; velocity (or speed); line; velocity (or speed); force
2nd: force; speed; mass; acceleration
3rd: action; equal; opposite

1. first
2. third
3. first
4. second
5. second
6. third
7. second
8. second
9. third
10. first

Page 29

1. inertia
2. friction
3. centripetal force
4. velocity
5. friction
6. gravity
7. air resistance or friction
8. momentum
9. friction
10. inertia
11. centripetal force
12. Inertia
13. acceleration
14. air resistance
15. rate

Page 30

1. 1.6 hours
2. 3.5 hours
3. yes; no
4. *Black Giant*
5. 9 P.M. central time
6. 115 mph
7. 5 mph
8. 100 mph
9. 1020 miles
10. *Chicago Skyscraper;* 152 miles farther

Page 31

I. Should include these three. Order is not important.

CONDUCTION: transfer of energy from particle to particle through matter. Particles at higher temperatures have more energy and vibrate further. They collide with cooler air and spread energy through the material. Heat travels by conduction mainly through solids.

CONVECTION: transfer of energy by the movement of the material, particularly in gases and liquids because they flow. When a fluid (gas or liquid) is heated, it becomes less dense and it is pushed upwards by cooler, more dense fluids that sink. This causes a current that moves heat.

RADIATION: transfer of energy that doesn't need matter. Source of radiant energy is mostly the sun. Radiant energy can travel through space where there is no matter.

II. Answers will vary somewhat.

1. Conduction and convection: Heat from the burner warms the pan by conduction. The liquid soup is warmed by convection currents.
2. The cooler has insulating material—something that is a poor conductor and does not allow thermal energy to transfer well.
3. Black absorbs radiant energy from the sun. White or shiny objects reflect the sun's energy.
4. by radiation
5. Metal is a good conductor of heat. The heat energy moves from the hot liquid through the spoon by conduction.
6. Plastic is a poor conductor of heat energy.
7. Houses are usually insulated with materials that do not transfer thermal energy well. Heat usually flows from warmest spot to cooler spots. The insulating materials hold the heat into the house.
8. The warmth travels through the air by convection.
9. When you wear layers, air is trapped between the layers. Your body heat warms these many pockets of air, and they add extra insulation to keep in your body heat.
10. Wood is a poor conductor of heat; this is a protection to keep hands from burning.
11. Conduction and convection: Heat energy outside the can warms the metal can (a good conductor) by conduction. Warmth from the surface of the can then transfers through the liquid by convection.
12. Microwaves carry radiant energy to the food. This causes the molecules in the food to vibrate rapidly and produce thermal energy (heat).

13. A solar heating system includes containers that store the heat collected on a sunny day. This heat is stored in such materials as hot water or stones.
14. A refrigerator is a heat mover because it removes heat from the food inside a cool space and puts the heat out into the room at a higher temperature (warm air comes out of the back of the refrigerator).
15. Extra heat in the environment is called thermal pollution because it can raise the temperature of the environment and change the ecosystem, causing danger to some life forms.
16. Dirt in the snow is dark in color and absorbs radiant energy from the sun. This causes the snow to melt. Clean snow reflects more of the sun's heat energy away.
17. Air is heated by convection. Warm air is always less dense and lighter. Heavier, denser, cooler air sinks and pushes warmer air upward.

Pages 32-33

1. friction
2. friction
3. kinetic
4. potential
5. inertia
6. kinetic
7. gravity
8. kinetic
9. potential
10. potential
11. potential
12. kinetic
13. potential
14. potential
15. potential (mechanical allowed also)
16. thermal

17. neither; they will both reach the ground at the same time, because gravity exerts the same pull on all objects, no matter what their mass
18. rock; air resistance will slow the feather more than the rock
19. Earth; pull of Earth's gravity is less strong on the moon
20. none, because the astronaut has the same mass, no matter where she is

Pages 34-35

I. A. transfer of energy as the result of the motion of objects
   B. a device that makes work easier
   C. a machine consisting of only one part
   D. number of times a machine multiplies an effort force
   E. force exerted by a machine
   F. force applied to the machine

II. Explanations of machines may vary.
   1. Lever: a bar that pivots on a fixed point
      a. fulcrum; b. effort force; c. resistance force
   2. Pulley: wheel that changes the direction of the effort force

3. Wheel & Axle: large wheel fixed to a smaller wheel or a bar called an axle
4. Inclined Plane: slanted surface used to raise objects
5. Wedge: an inclined plane with one or two sloping sides
6. Screw: an inclined plane wound around a cylinder, usually with a sharp ridge along the edge

III.
1. lever
2. wheel & axle
3. wedge
4. inclined plane
5. pulley
6. lever
7. lever
8. pulley
9. lever
10. wedge
11. screw
12. lever
13. wheel & axle
14. inclined plane
15. wedge
16. lever
17. screw
18. inclined plane
19. lever
20. wheel & axle

Page 36

1. wavelength
2. X
3. Y
4. frequency
5. velocity
6. higher
7. amplitude
8. transverse
9. compressional
10. electromagnetic
11. velocity
12. vibrations
13. hertz; one wave per second
14. 2

Page 37

1. transverse
2. radiation
3. frequencies
4. spectrum
5. visible
6. ultraviolet
7. 102 million waves pass a given point each second
8. X-rays
9. higher
10. TV
11. no
12. 56 Hz
13. radar
14. cosmic

Page 38

Answers may vary somewhat.
1. unit to measure the volume or loudness of sound
2. having to do with the amplitude of a sound wave
3. has a large amplitude
4. has a small amplitude
5. greatest distance a point on a sound wave travels from its rest position
6. a person's response to sound intensity; a sound wave with a large amplitude
7. sounds with pleasing tone quality and pitch

8. a quality of a sound determined by its frequency
9. sound with higher frequency
10. sound with lower frequency
11. differences among sounds of the same pitch and loudness
12. study of the science of sound
13. speed at which sound waves travel through a material or air
14. number of sound waves that pass a point at a given time
15. a change in wave frequency that is caused by the motion of the sound source or the motion of the person hearing it
16. sounds produced by irregular vibrations
17. mixture of many different sounds reflected

Page 39

1. A
2. A
3. B
4. D
5. C
6. Tim's
7. E
8. E
9. They are farther apart.
10. H
11. Pitch gets lower.
12. Pitch will become louder or higher.

Page 40

A. 11	E. 15	I. 8	M. 5
B. 4	F. 3	J. 16	N. 7
C. 6	G. 13	K. 9	O. 10
D. 12	H. 1	L. 2	P. 14

Page 41

1. The process of drying clothes in a dryer often causes them to gain an electric charge. This means that some of the atoms have too many or too few electrons. These atoms with too few and too many electrons attract each other, causing static electricity.
2. Drops of moisture in the air act as conductors to carry electricity across the air.
3. The skin of an electric eel has hundreds of cells that charge up like batteries and hold electric energy.
4. The power of wind can be used to turn a generator and produce electricity.
5. Rubbing a balloon against a sweater can cause some of the atoms in the sweater to lose and be transferred to the balloon. The electrons with too many or too few electrons attract each other, producing static electricity.
6. The comb passing through your hair causes some electrons to be transferred to the comb. The atoms with too few or too many electrons, then, attract each other, producing static electricity.

7. A glow worm produces light through a chemical process that takes place in its body.

8. Feet shuffling across a carpet causes some of the electrons from some atoms to be transferred between objects. The atoms with too few or too many electrons, then, attract each other and produce static electricity.

9. The human body has a complex nervous system that works with electric signals. The electricity is produced through chemical processes in the body.

10. The power of running water can be used to turn a generator and produce electricity.

Page 42

I. A. the flow of charged particles through a conductor
   B. alternating current: flow of particles constantly changing direction
   C. direct current: flow of particles in one direction

II. 1. A, B, C, D   4. C   7. 0
    2. E, F   5. B, E
    3. D   6. 2

8. Answers will vary somewhat: because your finger completes a circuit and makes a path for the electricity to flow—it conducts electricity through your body

Page 43

1. 1560 watts	5. 220 V
2. 12.5 A	6. 75.6 watts
3. 150 watts	7. 3.5 A
4. 120 V	8. 0.06 A

Page 44

Clues will vary somewhat but should contain generally this information:
Across
1. caused by a wave bouncing off an object
5. the bending of waves of light passing from one material into another
6. an object that refracts light twice and produces a visible spectrum
11. Light is a part of this spectrum of waves.
12. material that absorbs light
14. light waves that strike an object
15. color of unseparated light
Down
1. image that can be projected onto a screen
2. material that you can see through
3. bending of light waves as they pass through an opening or around a bend

4. visible part of the electromagnetic spectrum
6. instrument for seeing things not in the line of vision
7. colored bands of visible light
8. colored material that absorbs some colors and reflects others
9. material light passes through but cannot be seen through
10. instrument that uses light to see distant objects
13. ___ of incidence = ___ of refraction

Page 45

1. Only the red waves of the spectrum are reflected off red apples.
2. Pigments are added to paint to give them color. These pigments are colored liquids that absorb some colors and reflect others.
3. Something is black because it reflects no waves from the light spectrum.
4. Something appears white because it reflects all the colors in light together.
5. A prism, because of the angles in the glass, bends the white light. The different colors are refracted at different angles, and so the colors are separated out into a visible spectrum.
6. Raindrops act like tiny prisms. When the sun shines on the raindrops at a certain angle, the raindrops split the light into its many colors.
7. The water bends the light that is reflecting the image of the coin back to you.
8. Sunlight coming through Earth's atmosphere is reflected, or scattered, by millions of dust and water particles in the air. The shortest wavelengths of light are scattered more than the other wavelengths. These are the blue wavelengths. The dust and water scatter so many of these short wavelengths and scatter so much blue light that the sky appears blue.
9. Sunlight, low on the horizon, passes through a thicker layer of atmosphere. Most of the shorter wavelengths (blues and greens) are scattered out, leaving the longer wavelengths toward the red end of the light spectrum. This is why the sky appears red.
10. The indigo wavelengths are difficult to see. Only 1 person in every 1000 can see them.

Page 46

1. C	5. F	9. E
2. J	6. D	10. H
3. A	7. G	11. K
4. I	8. B	

Page 47

1. angle	11. 45°
2. thicker	12. Light
3. together	13. mirror
4. focal	14. mirror
5. focus	15. out of the line of vision
6. larger	16. aperture
7. thinner	17. lens
8. away	18. image
9. focus	19. film
10. mirror	20. inverted

Page 48

These are the corrected false answers. All other answers are true.

1. Magnetic poles that are UNLIKE attract.
6. One end will point NORTH, the other SOUTH.
8. Both ends have equal force.
10. The core is a piece of IRON.
14. Iron is NOT a permanent magnet.
16. Magnetic poles that are ALIKE REPEL one another . . . or . . . magnetic poles that are DIFFERENT ATTRACT each other.

Page 49

Words in puzzle:

acceleration	mass
acid	mixture
atom	molecule
current	motion
catalyst	nucleus
circuit	opaque
compound	parallel
condensation	pitch
Doppler	proton
electricity	radiation
electron	solution
element	static
formula	thermal
frequency	transparent
fulcrum	trough
gravity	velocity
hertz	volt
insulation	watt
kinetic	wavelength
lever	wedge
machine	work

Definition answers will vary depending on which words students choose to define.

Page 50

Answers will vary.